Great Canadian Ckies

PAMELA STEEL

XMAS 2003

**Prentice
Hall
Canada**

A Pearson Company
Toronto

Lucy

Canadian Cataloguing in Publication Data

Steel, Pamela
  Great Canadian Cookies

Includes index.
ISBN 0-13-031106-5

1. Cookies. I. Title.

TX772.S85 2000   641.8'654   C00-931466-0

ISBN 0-13-031106-5

Editorial Director, Trade Division: Andrea Crozier
Acquisitions Editor: Nicole de Montbrun
Copy Editor: Ruth Pincoe
Production Editor: Lori McLellan
Art Direction: Mary Opper
Cover and Interior Design: Mary Opper
Cover Photography: Per Kristiansen
Front Cover cookies baked by Sharon Houston
Production Manager: Kathrine Pummell
Page Layout: Arlene Edgar

1 2 3 4 5   KR   04 03 02 01 00

Printed and bound in Canada.

Visit the Prentice Hall Canada Web site!
Send us your comments, browse our catalogues,
and more. www.phcanada.com

Prentice
Hall
Canada

A Pearson Company

For Nathan

Contents

Chocolate Chip Cookies 1

Peanuts! 17

A Taste of the West 25
Cookies Recipes from British Columbia, Alberta, Saskatchewan, and Manitoba

Acknowledgments

Thanks to Ed Carson at Prentice Hall Canada who provided the creative spark that started this project cooking, and also to Nicole de Montbrun and the whole Prentice Hall editorial and production team for their great work. My thanks also to Kathy English of Canadian Online Explorer (CANOE) for holding the Great Canadian Cookie Contest and to Dr. Elsayed Abdelaal of Agriculture and Agrifood Canada for sharing his wealth of baking knowledge.

Special thanks go to my chef husband, Bill, for contributing his great skill, expertise, and culinary creativity to this book. My thanks also to my other kitchen assistants: Carolyn Hurren and Carol Steel, who spent long afternoons baking with me in my kitchen, and my son Nathan and his friends Mark Gasior and Monica Pawlowski, who were enthusiastic tasters.

I extend heartfelt gratitude to a number of marvelous women who also happen to be great cooks and who generously allowed me to reprint recipes from their excellent cookbooks: Julian Armstrong, Elizabeth Baird, Rose Murray, and Micheline Mongrain. Thanks also to Gary MacDougall, managing editor of the Charlottetown *Guardian*, for granting permission to use recipes from the Island Christmas Web site and to Barbara Barnes, supervisor and home economist at The Blue Flame Kitchen™ in Edmonton, for allowing me pass on three recipes as well as their excellent tips for sending cookies by mail.

And last, but by no means least, my sincere thanks to all the home cooks and professional bakers across the country who graciously offered their own recipes — you have provided heart and soul for this book.

Introduction

It all begins with teething biscuits. Our love of cookies starts in infancy and continues throughout our lives. Our taste may change from arrowroot to cappuccino macadamia cookies, but the basic longing for a sweet morsel remains the same. If you ask any small child where cookies come from, they won't understand the question. For them, cookies simply exist, like the sun and the moon and grandma. As long as there have been grandmothers to bake there have been cookies, and grandchildren to eat them.

There is no happier time than that moment of anticipation when a batch of cookies has come hot from the oven and you are waiting for them to cool just enough so you won't burn your mouth. Then the first bite … chocolate chips warm and gooey on your tongue, and the sweet, soft cakelike texture of the cookie, yielding and delicious — delightful!

I have not always been able to bake. As a beginning chef, I informed the world that I was inflicted with a baking curse. For some unknown reason, nothing I baked came out. I now believe that the problem lay in the intrinsic difference between baking and cooking. Cooking is a craft — and sometimes an art — that allows a lot of leeway for sudden bursts of inspiration. A dash of this, a splash of that, and a dish comes together. Baking is more of a science. Weights and measures must be exact. Oven positioning, evenness of temperature, and even altitude can have a tremendous effect on the finished product. Over the years, I have set myself to learn this science and happily, the baking curse has lifted. If you understand the principles of baking, — the science behind the cookie — you can make perfect cookies every time, and you can even invent your own recipes. See page xiv for all the information you need.

The 195 recipes in this book come from a variety of sources. The majority are either new recipes that were invented or classic recipes that were refined by my chef husband and me in our test kitchen. Our results were offered for tasting to the hoard of neighborhood children who have come to know our home as the "Cookie House." Believe me, children are refreshingly honest with their opinions. The remaining recipes come from pastry chefs, restaurants, B&Bs, culinary academies, and home cooks across Canada.

We also held a cookie contest on Canadian Online Explorer (CANOE) during which talented amateur from across the country submitted their favourite recipes. Choosing a winner was difficult because so many of the recipes were fantastic. See "The Great Canadian Cookie Contest" (pp. 65–95) for the winning recipe and a selection of the best entries.

Finally, we made an informal survey and discovered the one cookie which is an overwhelming favourite. For this reason, we have devoted an entire chapter to the art of the chocolate chip cookie. The second favourite turned out to be the unassuming peanut butter cookie, so there is also a chapter for lovers of that rich legume.

The range of cookies is large and the recipes for squares cover everything from the standard date and pecan to Rose Murray's Sensational Turtle Brownies. I hope you will find your favourite cookie somewhere in these pages. I thoroughly enjoyed writing this book and talking to cooks and bakers from across the country about one thing we all agree on — we love cookies!

The History of the Cookie

It is not possible to identify the very first cookie maker. Sweet baked morsels have been popular since antiquity when manna was gathered and baked into small breads. Modern cookie baking, however, has everything to do with the refinement and availability of sugar.

It is likely that one of the earliest cultures to enjoy baked sweets was Persia, where evidence of solid sugar production dates back to about 500 BC. Also, the further refinement of cane sugar was first accomplished in Persia during the seventh century and this extremely expensive and valued product soon made its way into western European countries.

By the thirteenth century there was a guild of cookie makers in Paris, and this guild was further regulated by King Charles the VI of France around the turn of the fifteenth century. Still it wasn't until the beginning of the nineteenth century that sugar became inexpensive enough to be widely used by home cooks.

The English word *biscuit*, comes from the French "biscuit" meaning twice cooked. The original Reims biscuit was a flat cake that was stored in a tin, then baked again to improve its shelf life. A similar hard, dry, cake that served as a sustaining food for soldiers and sailors dating back to the Roman Empire was called Parthian bread. In England, the word "biscuit" is used to describe a sweet, crisp wafer — think of Pimms.

The word "cookie" is distinctly North American, and it first appeared around the turn of the eighteenth century. It is derived from the Dutch word *koekje*, the "little cakes" that the early Dutch settlers brought from their homeland. Just as immigration changed the face of Canada, it also affected the cookie — variations of different sweet biscuits came from many of the emerging cultures.

However, these yummy little treats were not yet the ready booty of every passing child. No, cookies were an occasional indulgence, brought out as a special delight for festivals and celebrations.

It wasn't until the twentieth century that home cooks had the time and the resources to produce a steady supply of cookies. The facilities available in modern kitchens and easy access to ingredients such as sugar and butter helped the cookie to become the pop star it is today. One of our favourite cookies — the chocolate chip cookie — was invented by Ruth Wakefield in her kitchen at the Toll House Inn in Whitman, Massachusetts. The Toll House Cookie became the blueprint for countless variations of North America's most loved cookie.

It's interesting that while sweet biscuits have an ancient heritage, the cookie as we know it is a relatively new invention. Family recipes that go back a few generations are really original works of art. I am thinking of women such as my Grandma Gladys and her unbeatable date oatmeal cookies. When she devised this recipe in her cosy little kitchen, she created something new and wonderful in the culinary world. Congratulations to my grandma and to yours, and also to a century of home bakers for their ingenuity and creativity. Of all the gifts they have handed down to us, the cookie is certainly one that will endure.

The Science behind the Cookie

Cookies and science may seem like an odd combination, but nothing could be more natural. Baking is an exact science and every baker is a chemist. The chemical reactions that account for the leavening, the structure, and the composition of baked goods follow exact rules. We remember our grandmother's baking — she never used a recipe and she knew if the dough was right by the "feel" — without realizing that she was an accomplished chemist. Perhaps she didn't know why her recipes worked, but she knew the right steps to a successful cookie "experiment."

You may be perfectly happy following a few tried-and-true recipes — perhaps some of your grandmother's — but once you understand the science behind the cookie — why the cookie crumbles — few recipes will be beyond your grasp. In fact, you will have the skills to invent your own recipes. Most cookies are the product of the same basic steps. In this chapter I will explain the reasoning behind these steps.

The essential nature of a cookie can be described by the relationship of three ingredients: flour, fat and sugar. Measurements of these three ingredients break down to a ratio of 1:.40:.45. This means that for every cup of flour you put in your dough, you should put in about 2/5 of a cup of butter and a 1/2 cup sugar.

During my research for this chapter I interviewed Dr. Elsayed Abdelaal, a research scientist with the Agriculture and Agrifood Canada Food Research Program at the University of Guelph. Dr. Abdelaal is a cereal scientist who did his Ph.D. studies in bread and baking, working with soft wheat, cookies, cakes, and pastries. He was extremely generous with his time and I have included a number of his comments in the following paragraphs.

Most recipes follow the same basic steps. Let's examine them one by one.

1. Cream together the butter and sugar(s) until they are light and fluffy.

Unless otherwise specified, *soft butter should be used for all recipes in this book*. Allow butter to soften at room temperature for about 45 minutes. To test it, press your finger gently into the butter. Your finger should leave a slight indentation. If the butter is too soft and beginning to melt, the dough will not have enough structure and will spread too much during baking.

I do not recommend substituting margarine or hydrogenated vegetable spreads for butter, primarily because a cookie made with butter will always taste infinitely nicer than one made with margarine. Also, since there are suspected health risks associated with hydrogenated oils, I do not cook with them. Shortening is often used for cookies, and many commercial bakers prefer its smooth, moist texture, but it still lacks the flavour that only butter can provide.

The "creaming" process is a must for soft, chewy cookies because it incorporates air into the dough; it is the first step in a process that requires little mixing once the flour is added. The reason for this is that the gluten — the protein in flour that helps with leavening — will cause toughness in baked goods if it is overworked. If mixing is kept to a minimum after the flour is added, the result will be a more tender product.

Sugar crystals have sharp edges that can be seen under a microscope. These edges cut into the solid fat and create air cells. If you use butter that is too soft, these pockets of air will have nothing to hang on to. This is why the butter must be just soft enough to cream.

Both the butter and the sugar contribute to the moisture in cookies. The butter — the fat in the cookie — accounts for the characteristic moist, smooth mouth feel. Sugar is hygroscopic — that is, it absorbs moisture — so even though it is a dry ingredient, it actually helps to make the cookie more moist. Fat and sugar also work together to keep the cookie tender by separating the starch of the flour from the coagulated protein in the fat.

According to Dr. Abdelaal: "In cakes and cookies, the creaming process incorporates air cells into the system and provides a fluffy, fine and soft texture. Sugar and fat, when combined by creaming, incorporate air into the fat so the air cells are more stable. Because the air cells are protected by the fat the cookie dough can sit for extended periods of time without compromising the fluffy structure." Hmmm... so that's why cookies stay fresh longer than bread.

2. Beat in eggs and vanilla or other flavourings.

Eggs contribute moisture, fat, and protein to the dough. Cookies require less moisture than any other pastry or bread. Usually eggs and vanilla extract are the only suppliers of water. The protein in egg adds to the structure of the cookie and the fat contributes tenderness and moisture. In cookies such as macaroons, egg whites are whipped. This traps air and gives the cookie its structure. Eggs do add taste to the cookie, but as with salt and baking powder, you don't actually want to be able to identify the egg taste. An "eggy" cookie is not a pleasant thing.

Usually, eggs are beaten into the dough one at time, and are followed by the flavourings. At this early stage the dough ingredients should be really well mixed. Dr. Abdelaal says: "Again, we are incorporating air into the system for the fluffy texture in the end product. Air is trapped in both the fat and in the white of eggs. We beat the eggs to incorporate more air into the egg white. Usually eggs have a smell we don't like. Flavourings cover this eggy smell and taste."

I recommend using pure vanilla extract rather than artificial vanilla for the taste. The same goes for all flavourings — better quality ingredients will result in a more pleasant product.

3. Sift or mix together flour, baking powder or soda, salt, and any spices.

The dry ingredients should be thoroughly mixed together before they are added to the wet ingredients. Once flour is combined with moisture, overdevelopment of gluten, and the resulting toughness, becomes a problem.

On the subject of baking powder and soda, in his fascinating book, *On Food and Cooking: The Science and Lore of the Kitchen*, Harold McGee tells us that, "the mixture of an acid with an alkali to produce carbon dioxide gas was developed around 1835 in England, and commercial baking powders first appeared around 1850. Chemical leavenings exploit the reaction between certain acidic and alkaline compounds, which results in the evolution of carbon dioxide, the same gas that yeast produces." This carbon dioxide creates bubbles in the batter as it cooks.

Yeast is a powerful leavening agent capable of leavening bread, but it has more strength than than we want for a cookie, which is a much denser product. We do, however, want some lightness in the cookie and baking powders accomplish this. Baking soda (sodium bicarbonate) is an alkaline and will work by itself in dough that already contains acid from sour milk, yogurt, lemon juice, or vinegar.

"Baking powder," McGee writes, "contains baking soda and an acid in the form of salt crystals that dissolve in water. Most are double acting; that is they produce an initial set of gas bubbles upon mixing and a second set during baking." There are two types of acid salts in baking powder: one is activated at room temperature and the other at the higher temperature of the oven. What this means, is that the dough is lightened by one set of bubbles during mixing and by a second just before setting in the oven.

Baking soda is four times as powerful as baking powder. If you have run out of baking powder and are making a dough that has no additional acidic ingredients, combine 1/2 tsp (2ml) cream of tartar with 1/4 teaspoon (1ml) baking soda and substitute for 1 tsp (5ml) baking powder.

It is important to mix baking powder or soda well into the flour in order to prevent lumps or areas where the chemical is highly concentrated. The nasty taste you sometimes get with chemical leaveners is caused either by using too much baking soda or powder or by improper mixing.

A little bit of salt is added to cookie dough to enhance flavour, but you should never be able to actually taste the salt in the finished product.

All-purpose flour, a blend of hard and soft flours, contains a median amount of protein (about 10.5 percent) and is best for most cookies. Harder flour (bread flour) has a higher protein content and thus contains more gluten, resulting in a chewier, tougher product (which is why it is used for bread). Pastry flour has a lower protein content and thus contains less gluten. It cannot provide the structure needed for most types of cookies, but it is ideally suited to delicate cakes and pastries.

As we have said, baking is a science. An important part of ensuring a successful cookie experiment is proper measuring techniques. Scoop flour and other dry ingredients into dry measures and level the top using the flat side of a knife.

As for the relative value of sifting or simply mixing, Dr. Abdelaal says, "Each baker to their own preferred method. If we sift, we get a uniform fine size of ingredient, which best distributes these particles in a uniform system — it homogenizes all the dry material in the recipe. The finer the particle size of the ingredient the better the quality of the product. In industry, we try to get the finest quality soft wheat flour: 7 to 9 percent. If you try to reduce the particle size you can damage the starch granules and damaged starch will adversely effect the quality of cookies."

4. Stir flour mixture into the creamed butter in thirds.

Again, a successful cookie dough is well mixed but not overmixed. If you add the flour a little at a time, you can mix evenly without too much stirring. Stirring in by hand, rather than with a mechanical device, also helps to minimize the manipulation of the dough.

On this subject, Dr. Abdelaal says, "The goal is to produce a uniform mixture of short dough. Cookie dough should be a cohesive mass but if you stretch it, it breaks — it has no elasticity, no resistance to stretching. The low moisture content of cookie dough does not allow the gluten to develop — a necessary thing for bread, but not for cookies. The degree of gluten development depends both on the amount of moisture and on the amount of mixing time and energy. For a sheet cookie that you cut, you need a little more water so you can form the sheet. Sheet cookies actually need more gluten development than drop cookies."

5. Fold in additional ingredients such as chocolate chips, nuts, or toffee.

The dough has its structure and is well mixed. Now it is time to add the goodies. These should be folded in gently so they are dispersed throughout the dough without too much additional working of the gluten in the flour.

6. Refrigerate the dough.

Sometimes, but not always, the dough is refrigerated. This accomplishes two things. First, it makes the dough harder. In the case of some sticky doughs, this hardness is necessary to shape the cookies. For rolled cookies, chilling the dough makes it much easier to roll and cut. Secondly, cooling the dough will help the cookies to hold their shape during baking.

According to Dr. Abdelaal, "This allows the system to rest but with the limited amount of water in the dough, there is very little interaction. I don't know the scientific reason behind this step — it's an example of the art in cookie baking. Chilling the dough, I think, has something to do with the fat and sugar in the system. Once the cookie goes into the oven, both the fat and the sugar start to melt, they become soluble — and there you have the fluidity of the dough. By chilling the dough, you can delay this fluidity for awhile, and this delays the spreading. However, I have no scientific evidence for my opinion. The viscosity may change — this is something to experiment with."

7. Preheat the oven.

An even heat has everything to do with successful cookie baking. The oven should be up to temperature before you put the cookies in. For most cookies, I prefer a moderate oven, about 325ºF to 375ºF (160ºC to 190ºC). A hotter oven will seal the outside of the cookie and may even burn it before the inside is fully cooked. A cooler oven, on the other hand will result in a hard cookie.

Dr. Abdelaal says, "At a lower temperature you would have to bake the cookies for a long time. A very hard texture results because of the many reactions that occur. An even heat avoids adverse effects. Too high an oven temperature accelerates the rate of action for browning, hardening and caramelization, leaving the inside of the cookie undercooked.

8. Prepare the cookie sheet.

Cookie sheets are a question of individual preference. However, since even heat is an important issue, it pays to give some attention to the cookie sheet. A dark sheet will attract heat. This results in overcooking the bottom of the cookie, making it hard or even burned. A reflective surface will reflect heat. This reflection helps to ensure that the top and bottom of the cookie bake evenly. However, I haven't thrown away my old, black cookie sheets — I just cover them with parchment paper. I have also experimented with the new air sheets and clay sheets, both of which are intended to assure even heat and foolproof baking. I like the air sheets — the cookies baked nicely — but I found that with the clay sheets the cookies were actually undercooked on the bottom and often hollow in the centre.

There are three basic ways to prepare a cookie sheet. The method of preparation depends on the type of cookie. Ungreased sheets are generally used for cookies that have enough fat in the dough to prevent sticking. An ungreased sheet will also help cookies to keep their shape. However, if you want the cookies to spread, greasing is the best option. Greased sheets will give a thinner, crisper cookie. Parchment lined sheets are my personal favourite: the cookies don't burn on the bottom, they don't stick, and they hold their shape.

Finally, be sure to fill the tray. We're back to even heat here. Every small change in the oven affects the result of your "experiment." The number of cookies on the sheet and the distances between each one will affect the evenness of the heat to which each cookie is exposed.

9. Bake on the middle rack of the oven.

This is yet another precaution to ensure that perfect even heat we're seeking. On the middle rack of the oven, the cookies are exposed to the same amount of heat above and below, and the heat can circulate freely around the cookie sheet.

10. Bake for 8 to 15 minutes.

Yes, some recipes require longer baking times, depending on size and composition of the cookies, but 8 to 15 minutes covers the majority of recipes — long enough to give the outside of the cookie a firm, golden to brown coat, but short enough to ensure that the inside is cooked but still moist and chewy. On this subject Dr. Abdelaal says. "Baking is an economic process for cookies because of the lack of water. With bread you have to cook off the water to dry it up, but with cookies there is very little water, so they cook quickly."

11. Check for doneness at the minimum time.

Checking for doneness is usually a visual process. Look for a golden bottom and edges or a general browning. You can also check doneness by feel. Some cookies should spring back when lightly touched, and the dough should be just set. You can often check squares by inserting a toothpick: if it comes out dry then you know the squares have set through to the centre.

According to Dr. Abdelaal, "The brown colour of your product can be used as an indication of complete baking. The browning action in the baking occurs between the sugar and the amino acids in the proteins — they act together to create the brown colour. Coloured and flavoured compounds are a result of the browning reaction. The product undergoes this browning reaction in baking, so once we have the brown colour it means the product has gone through all of the physical and chemical reactions necessary to a successful product. The brown colour is, however, only one indication. Texture is more important — we are looking for the tender bite."

12. Transfer to Cooling Racks.

Allow the cookies to cool on the cookie sheet for up to two minutes before moving them to cooling racks. This will help the cookies to hold their structure. Cooling racks provide an even dissipation of heat. It is important to allow cooler air to circulate all around the cookie in order to stop the cooking process. As long as the cookies are hot, they will continue to cook. The transfer to cooling racks also eliminates the problem of having cookies stuck to the cookie sheet. Dr. Abdelaal says, "You need a cooling system to eliminate the heat — this stops the cooking process. As long as the cookie is hot the browning reaction and all actions continue. Transferring the cookie to a cooling rack stops overcooking or overbaking."

Storing Cookies

Most of the recipes in this book don't mention storing cookies. The methods are simple, and they depend on the type of cookie. A crisp cookie needs to stay dry and will survive best in a cookie jar or tin. A chewy cookie needs to retain its moisture and it will survive best in an airtight container with a piece of bread.

Almost all cookies taste best when they are fresh, but most will keep for a few days at room temperature and for a few weeks in the freezer. Do not store cookies in the refrigerator — temperatures that are suitable for storing perishable foods are death to pastries and breads. Have you ever noticed how hard a loaf of bread becomes after a few hours in the refrigerator? I asked Dr. Abdelaal why refrigeration is so bad for cookies. "Because of the high starch content, the rate of firming of baked goods is higher at lower temperatures. If you heat a piece of glass it converts to a rubber material and given more heat it becomes flowable, but once you cool it down you have glass again. It's the same with a bakery product. A piece of bread from the oven is fresh, tasty and the surface is very dry — the hard texture of the product will change from hard and dry to a rubbery state at a lower temperature, like that found in a refrigerator. The firming process goes on at room temperature, but at a slower rate."

I also asked Dr. Abdelaal why cookie dough, and even baked cookies can be frozen so successfully. He replied, "Because of the low moisture content. When you freeze any system — tissue or food — you freeze the water inside the system. When the water converts from a liquid state to a crystal state, the size and shape of the crystals can damage the system. Less water means fewer crystals, so less chance of damage. So, there are no adverse effects on the product. Again, this is from experience and not from scientific evidence."

Cookie dough can be frozen either in batches or in individual portions for easy baking. I like to portion the dough, freeze it on a cookie tray until firm. and then transfer the unbaked cookies to an airtight freezer bag. This means I can then bake the cookies in small batches.

In our house, the number of cookies baked in a given day is exactly the same as the number of cookies eaten on that day. If I want to control my family's intake of cookies, I find it's best to bake one tray at a time. As discussed earlier, for even baking the cookie tray should be full, so it's not a good idea to bake partial trays. You can, however, buy a small cookie tray that holds about eight cookies — perfect for a family of four.

Cookie Commandments

There are a number of universal rules for successful cookie baking.
Follow them and you will be transformed from a baking
washout to a cookie wizard!

**Always preheat the oven. Use an oven thermometer to make sure the
temperature is correct. Many ovens run hot or cold.**

•

**All ingredients should be at room temperature. If eggs are cold,
run them under warm water for a few minutes.**

•

**Butter must be soft. To check, press your finger on the top — it should
leave a slight indentation.**

•

**Spend an extra few minutes creaming the butter and sugar. The more
air you incorporate at this stage, the better.**

•

Add eggs one at a time.

•

Use pure vanilla extract.

Measure dry ingredients by scooping them into dry measures
and levelling the top with the flat side of a knife.

•

Combine flour with leaveners and salt in a separate bowl.
Stir the flour mixture into the creamed mixture a third at a time.

•

Do not overmix the dough.

•

Once you have added the flour to the creamed ingredients,
mix by hand.

•

Use a reflective cookie sheet and prepare it as
specified in the instructions.

•

Space cookies on the sheet as directed in the recipe,
and fill each sheet evenly.

•

Bake cookies on the middle rack of the oven.

•

Check cookies after the shortest time specified in the recipe.
Most cookies should bake until they are golden
at the bottom and the edges.

•

Transfer hot cookies to a cooling rack for even cooling.

Chocolate Chip Cookies

It is fitting that the first recipe chapter is devoted entirely to the chocolate chip cookie. According to the results of both my own informal survey and a poll conducted by Canadian Online Explorer (CANOE), our favourite cookie by far is the chocolate chip. The first documented chocolate chip cookie was created by Ruth Wakefield for the enjoyment of guests at her Toll House Inn in Whitman, Massachusetts. This was some time before 1930 but this cookie has survived in its original form for more than seventy years. It has also been the subject of great creative tinkering.

Chocolate has several natural allies: nuts, raisins, mint, orange, and my favourite — coffee. Some of the recipes in this chapter celebrate these complementary tastes. Other old standards feature oatmeal and some interesting new spice combinations. Whatever your taste, I hope you will find the chocolate chip cookie of your dreams somewhere in these pages.

Raisin Chocolate Chip Cookies

*Perhaps the chocolate-covered raisins are overkill but when
it comes to cookies, I like to err in favour of excess.*

3/4 cup (175ml)	soft butter
1/2 cup (125ml)	granulated sugar
1 cup (250ml)	firmly packed brown sugar
2	eggs
3 tbsp (50 ml)	corn syrup
1 tsp (5ml)	vanilla
3 cups (750ml)	all-purpose flour
1 tsp (5ml)	baking powder
1/4 tsp (1ml)	baking soda
1/4 tsp (1ml)	salt
1 cup (250ml)	semi-sweet chocolate chips
1 1/2 cup (375ml)	chocolate-covered raisins

Preheat oven to 350ºF (180ºC).

Cream together butter and sugars until well combined. Beat in eggs, one at a time, then corn syrup and vanilla.

In a separate bowl, combine flour, baking powder, baking soda, and salt. Stir flour mixture into creamed mixture in thirds.

Drop heaping tablespoons of dough 3 inches (8cm) apart on a parchment-lined cookie sheet.

Bake on the middle rack of the oven for 18 to 20 minutes or until golden. Transfer to cooling racks.

Makes about 3 dozen cookies.

Mary Chapman's Chocolate Chip Mini Bites

*Mary, our neighbour in Waterloo, Ontario, bakes these cookies in
a mini-muffin pan because her three sons love the shape.*

1 cup (250ml)	soft butter
1 cup (250ml)	brown sugar
1 cup (250ml)	granulated sugar
2	eggs
2 tsp (10ml)	vanilla
2 tsp (10ml)	hot water
2 cups (500ml)	all-purpose flour
1 tsp (5ml)	baking soda
1 tsp (5ml)	salt
3/4 cup (175ml)	oatmeal
2 cups (500ml)	semi-sweet chocolate chips

Preheat oven to 325°F (160°C).

Cream together butter and sugars until light and fluffy. Beat in eggs, one at a time, then vanilla and water.

In a separate bowl, combine flour, baking soda, and salt. Stir in oatmeal. Stir flour mixture into creamed mixture in thirds. Fold in chocolate chips. Spoon batter into a greased mini muffin tins.

Bake on the middle rack of the oven for 8 minutes or until golden. Cool on sheets for 2 minutes then transfer to cooling racks.

Makes about 3 dozen cookie muffins.

Oatmeal Chocolatey Chip Cookies

*This recipe is from Carol Oberg, of Casey's Bed and Breakfast in Whitehorse, Yukon.
She writes, "When I put a plate of these down for an evening snack,
I never have any leftovers. Sometimes I mix up a large batch, freeze them at
the ball stage (on cookie sheets), and store them in plastic bags."*

2 1/2 cups (625ml)	oatmeal
1 cup (250ml)	soft butter
1 cup (250ml)	granulated sugar
1 cup (250ml)	brown sugar
2	eggs
1 tsp (5ml)	vanilla
2 cups (500ml)	all-purpose flour
1/2 tsp (2ml)	salt
1 tsp (5ml)	baking powder
1 tsp (5ml)	baking soda
1 3/4 cups (425ml)	chocolate chips
1 1/2 cups (375ml)	chopped, mixed nuts (walnuts, pecans, almonds)

Preheat oven to 375ºF (190º C).

Measure oatmeal into the bowl of a food processor and process until it is as fine as flour.

Cream together butter and sugars until light and fluffy. Beat in eggs and vanilla. In a separate bowl, mix together flour, salt, baking powder, and baking soda. Stir in oatmeal, chocolate chips, and nuts.

Stir flour mixture into butter mixture in thirds. Roll into 1-inch (2.5cm) balls and place 2 inches (5cm) apart on an ungreased cookie sheet.

Bake for 12 minutes or until golden.

Makes about 5 dozen cookies.

Oat Cookies with Chocolate Chips and Orange

*The combination of chocolate and orange — sweet and citrus —
contributes a nice layering of flavour. Talented home cooks, like good pastry chefs,
have a fine-tuned ability to build tastes from complementary foods.*

1 cup (250ml)	soft butter
1/2 cup (125ml)	brown sugar
1/2 cup (125ml)	granulated sugar
2	eggs
1 tsp (5ml)	vanilla
1 cup (250ml)	all-purpose flour
1/2 tsp (2ml)	baking soda
1/2 tsp (2ml)	salt
2 1/2 cups (625ml)	instant oats
1 cup (250ml)	chocolate chips
2 tbsp (25ml)	grated orange zest

Cream together butter and sugars until light and fluffy. Beat in eggs and vanilla. Sift together flour, baking soda, and salt. Stir in oats.

Stir flour mixture into creamed mixture until half combined. Add chips and orange and stir until all the ingredients are combined. Refrigerate dough for 1 hour.

Preheat oven to 325°F (160°C).

Roll dough into 1-inch (2.5 cm) balls, and place on an ungreased cookie sheet.

Bake for 10 minutes or until the edges are darkened.

Makes about 4 dozen cookies.

Chocolate Espresso Shortbread

Now we're talking! Chocolate and coffee —
especially good espresso — were meant for each other.

1 1/2 cups (375ml)	soft butter
3/4 cup (175ml)	sugar
1/4 cup (50ml)	espresso coffee
3 cups (750ml)	all-purpose flour
1/2 tsp (2ml)	salt
1 1/4 cups (300ml)	chocolate chips

Preheat oven to 350°F (180°C).

Cream together butter and sugar. Beat in coffee. Mix together flour and salt. Stir in chocolate chips. Mix dry ingredients into creamed butter in thirds.

Press dough into an 8-inch (2L) round cake pan. The dough will be 1/2 to 3/4 inch (1 to 2cm) thick.

Bake for 45 to 50 minutes or until edges are golden and top is dry. Cut into 1 1/2-inch (4cm) wedges and let cool.

Makes 18 to 24 wedges.

Spiced Chocolate Chip Cookies

Spices are best when they are fresh and fragrant. Purchase spices in small quantities and store them away from heat and light. Buy nutmeg whole and grate small amounts as needed — the difference in flavour is worth the few seconds of trouble.

2 cups (500ml)	all-purpose flour
1 tbsp (15ml)	cinnamon
1 tsp (5ml)	ground ginger
1/2 tsp (2ml)	freshly ground nutmeg
1/2 tsp (2ml)	baking powder
1/4 tsp (1ml)	salt
1 cup (250ml)	soft butter
1 cup (250ml)	packed brown sugar
1	egg
1 tsp (5ml)	vanilla
1/2 cup (125ml)	chocolate chips

Sift together flour, cinnamon, ginger, nutmeg, baking powder, and salt. In a separate bowl, cream butter and sugar until light and fluffy. Beat in egg and vanilla.

Stir flour mixture into creamed mixture in thirds. Fold in chocolate chips. Refrigerate for 2 hours.

Preheat oven to 350ºF (170ºC).

Roll dough into 1-inch (2.5cm) balls and place 2 inches (5cm) apart on a parchment-lined cookie sheet. Flatten each ball slightly with a fork dipped in cold water.

Bake on the middle rack of the oven for 12 to 15 minutes or until golden.

Makes about 3 dozen cookies.

Java Bean Cookies

For adults only! Chocolate-covered espresso beans replace chips in this eye opener designed for true coffee lovers.

1 cup (250ml)	soft butter
3/4 cup (175ml)	firmly packed brown sugar
1/2 cup (125ml)	granulated sugar
1	egg
1 tsp	(5ml) vanilla
1 3/4 cups (425ml)	all-purpose flour
1/2 tsp (2ml)	baking soda
1/4 tsp (1ml)	salt
1 cup (250ml)	chocolate-covered espresso beans

Preheat oven to 190ºC (375º F).

Cream together butter and sugars until light and fluffy. Beat in egg, then vanilla.

In a separate bowl, combine flour, baking soda, and salt. Stir flour mixture into creamed mixture in thirds. Fold in coffee beans.

Roll dough into 1 1/2-inch (4cm) balls and place 2 inches (5cm) apart on a parchment-lined cookie sheet.

Bake on the middle rack of the oven for 9 to 12 minutes or until golden. Transfer to cooling racks.

Makes about 2 dozen large cookies

Praline Chocolate Chunk Cookies

We usually think of pralines as caramel-coated almonds, but often I use a type made with mixed nuts. The variety of nuts lends a nice flavour dimension to this cookie. Cut chocolate chunks from solid blocks or one-ounce pieces of chocolate.

1 1/4 cups (300ml)	all-purpose flour
1/2 tsp (2ml)	baking soda
1/8 tsp (.5ml)	salt
1/2 cup (125 ml)	soft butter
3/4 cup (175ml)	packed brown sugar
1	egg
1 tsp (5ml)	vanilla
10 oz (300g)	chocolate chunks
1 1/2 cups (325ml)	chopped pralines

Preheat oven to 350°F (180°C).

Sift together flour, baking soda, and salt. In a separate bowl, cream butter and sugar until light and fluffy. Beat in egg and vanilla.

Stir flour mixture into creamed mixture in thirds. Fold in chocolate chunks and pralines. (The dough will be dry and crumbly.) Press dough into 1-inch (2.5cm) balls — do not flatten — and place 2 inches (5cm) apart on a parchment-lined cookie sheet.

Bake on middle rack of the oven for 10 to 12 minutes or until edges are browned. Cool on cookie sheets for 2 minutes, then transfer to cooling racks.

Makes about 4 dozen cookies.

Crispy Coconut Chocolate Chip Cookies

This recipe comes from Elli Stabile of Elli's B&B in Canmore, Alberta.
If you find the dough is too dry to work, add a splash of milk.

1 cup (250ml)	soft butter
1 1/2 cups (375ml)	brown sugar
1	egg
1 tsp (5ml)	vanilla
1 1/2 cups (375ml)	all-purpose flour
2 tsp (10ml)	baking powder
1/4 tsp (1ml)	baking soda
1/4 tsp (1ml)	salt
1 1/2 cups (375ml)	rolled oats
1 cup (250ml)	coconut
1 cup (250ml)	chocolate chips

Cream butter and sugar until light and fluffy. Beat in egg and vanilla. In a separate bowl, sift together flour, baking powder, baking soda, and salt.

Stir flour mixture into creamed mixture in thirds. In a food processor, process oats and coconut until the mixture resembles coarse crumbs. Fold oat mixture and chocolate chips into dough. Refrigerate for 1 hour.

Preheat oven to 350ºF (180ºC).

Form dough into 1-inch (2.5cm) balls and place 2 inches (5cm) apart on a greased cookie sheet.

Bake on the middle rack of the oven for 12 to 15 minutes or until golden. Cool on cookie sheet for 2 minutes, then transfer to cooling racks.

Makes about 3 dozen cookies.

Banana Chocolate Chip Cookies

Bananas are one of the few fruits that ripen after being picked. Single bananas are referred to as "fingers," and small bunches are called "hands."

1 cup (250ml)	soft butter
1 cup (250ml)	tightly packed brown sugar
2	eggs
1 tsp (5ml)	vanilla
1	very ripe banana
2 1/4 cups (550ml)	all-purpose flour
1/2 tsp (2ml)	baking powder
1/4 tsp (1ml)	salt
1/2 cup (125ml)	finely-ground dried banana
1 cup (250ml)	chocolate chips

Preheat oven to 375°F (190°C).

Cream together butter and sugars until light and fluffy. Beat in eggs, vanilla, and mashed banana. In a separate bowl, mix flour, baking powder, salt, and dried banana.

Stir flour mixture into creamed mixture in thirds. Fold in chocolate chips. Drop teaspoons of dough 2 inches (5cm) apart on a parchment-lined baking sheet.

Bake for 8 to 10 minutes or until edges are golden. Cool on cookie sheet for 2 minutes, then transfer to cooling rack.

Makes about 5 dozen cookies.

Cinnamon and Pepper Chocolate Chip Cookies

Here's another recipe designed to appeal to adult palates.
The black pepper gives this cookie a unique kick.

1 cup (250ml)	soft butter
1 cup (250ml)	firmly-packed brown sugar
2	eggs
1 tsp (5ml)	vanilla
3 cups (750ml)	all-purpose flour
1 tsp (5ml)	baking powder
1/2 tsp (2ml)	baking soda
1 tbsp (15ml)	ground cinnamon
1/4 tsp (1ml)	salt
1/8 tsp (.5ml)	ground black pepper
1 cup (250ml)	semi-sweet chocolate chips

Preheat oven to 180ºC (350º F).

Cream butter and sugar until light and fluffy. Beat in eggs, one at a time, and then vanilla.

In a separate bowl, mix together flour, baking powder, baking soda, cinnamon, salt, and pepper. Stir flour mixture into creamed mixture in thirds. Fold in chocolate chips.

Drop heaping teaspoons of dough 2 inches (5cm) apart on a greased cookie sheet. Flatten with a fork.

Bake for 10 to 12 minutes or until golden brown. Transfer to cooling racks.

Makes about 7 dozen cookies.

S'Mores

*For children, singing around the campfire has more to do
with marshmallows and s'mores than anything else. These treats bring
all the fun of a roaring fire to the kitchen.*

1 cup (250ml)	soft butter
1 cup (250ml)	sugar
2	eggs
1 tsp (5ml)	vanilla
2 cups (500ml)	all-purpose flour
1 cup (250ml)	graham cracker crumbs
1 tsp (5ml)	baking powder
3/4 cup (175ml)	semi-sweet chocolate chips
1 cup (250ml)	marshmallow spread

Preheat oven to 350ºF (180ºC).

Cream together butter and sugar until light and fluffy. Beat in eggs, one at a time, then add vanilla.

In a separate bowl, mix together flour, graham cracker crumbs, and baking powder. Stir flour mixture into creamed mixture in thirds. Fold in chocolate chips.

Drop heaping half-tablespoons of dough 2 inches (5cm) apart on a parchment-lined cookie sheet.

Bake on the middle rack of the oven for 15 to 18 minutes or until golden. Transfer to cooling racks.

Once cool, spread marshmallow on the bottom side of each cookie and sandwich two cookies together.

Makes about 3 dozen cookies.

Minty Chocolate Chip Cookies

Mint and chocolate — a natural flavour combination!
If fresh mint is not available, substitute a few drops of mint essence.

3/4 cup (175ml)	soft butter
1/2 cup (125ml)	granulated sugar
3/4 cup (175ml)	firmly packed golden sugar
1	egg
1 tsp (5ml)	vanilla
2 cups (500ml)	all-purpose flour
2 tbsp (10ml)	chopped fresh mint leaves
1 tsp (5ml)	baking powder
1/4 tsp (1ml)	salt
1 1/4 cups (300ml)	mint chocolate chips

Preheat oven to 350ºF (180ºC).

Cream together butter and sugars until light and fluffy. Beat in egg and vanilla. In a separate bowl, combine flour, mint, baking powder, and salt. Stir flour mixture into creamed mixture in thirds. Fold in chocolate chips.

Roll into 1-inch (2.5cm) balls, place 2 inches (5cm) apart on a parchment-lined cookie sheet, and flatten with the bottom of a glass.

Bake on the middle rack of the oven for 12 to 14 minutes or until golden. Transfer to cooling racks.

Makes about 4 dozen cookies.

Sour Cream Chocolate Chip Cookies

If you are concerned about the high-fat content of sour cream, you can substitute light sour cream in this recipe. (Don't use the nonfat variety because it contains stabilizers that will affect the consistency of the dough.)

1/2 cup (125ml)	soft butter
1 cup (250ml)	sugar
1	egg
1/4 cup (50ml)	sour cream
1 tsp (5ml)	vanilla
2 cups (500ml)	all-purpose flour
1/2 tsp (2ml)	baking soda
1/4 tsp (1ml)	salt
3/4 cup (175ml)	raisins
1/2 cup (125ml)	walnuts
3/4 cup (175ml)	chocolate chips

Preheat oven to 375ºF (190ºC).

Cream together butter and sugar until light and fluffy. Beat in eggs, sour cream, and vanilla. In a separate bowl, combine flour, baking soda, and salt.

Stir flour mixture into creamed mixture in thirds. Fold in raisins, walnuts, and chocolate chips. Drop tablespoons of batter 3 inches (8cm) apart on a parchment-lined cookie sheet.

Bake on the middle rack of the oven for 14 to 16 minutes or until the edges are golden.

Makes about 3 dozen cookies.

Maple Chocolate Chip Cookies

In early spring, we make a family visit to the Elmira Maple Syrup Festival in Ontario's Mennonite country. The day always features a foray into the sugar bush to watch maple syrup being made in a hundred-year-old sugar shack. Some of the maple syrup we bring home is used in these cookies.

1/2 cup (125ml)	soft butter
1/2 cup (125ml)	firmly packed brown sugar
1	egg
1 tsp (5ml)	vanilla
1/4 cup (50ml)	maple syrup
2 1/4 cups (550ml)	flour
1 tsp (5ml)	baking powder
1 tsp (5ml)	cinnamon
1/4 tsp (1ml)	salt
1/2 cup (125ml)	walnuts, chopped
1 cup (250ml)	semi-sweet chocolate chips

Preheat oven to 350ºF (180ºC).

Cream together butter and sugar until light and fluffy. Beat in egg, vanilla, and maple syrup. In a separate bowl, combine flour, baking powder, cinnamon, and salt. Fold in walnuts and chocolate chips.

Drop heaping tablespoons of batter 3 inches (8cm) apart on a parchment-lined cookie sheet. Flatten with the bottom of a glass.

Bake on the middle rack of the oven for 10 to 12 minutes or until golden. Transfer to cooling racks.

Makes about 3 dozen cookies.

Peanuts!

When we conducted our informal survey, we found that the chocolate chip cookie was the clear favourite, but running close on its heels was the peanut butter cookie. It was certainly the winner of my own cookie popularity contest when I was growing up.

My Grandma Gladys — queen of the peanut butter cookie — made those melt-in-your-mouth, bite-sized cookies with the trademark fork design on the top. Bite-sized cookies are definitely the mark of a dedicated home cook. Large cookies, now all the rage, are more the work of commercial cookie makers for whom small cookies are not cost effective. But really, isn't that little cookie just enough to satisfy a moment's craving perfectly? Of course, every time I passed at Grandma Gladys' cookie jar, another of those morsels would find its way into my greedy little fist.

I don't know who first thought of using peanut butter in a cookie, but I imagine it wasn't long after the introduction of this delicacy at the St. Louis World's Fair in 1904. The high fat content and rich, buttery taste of peanut butter make it a natural for cookies. Usually creamed with the butter, it adds texture, moisture, and full flavour to both the traditional peanut butter cookie and its modern variations.

Milk Chocolate Peanut Butter Cookies

This recipe comes from the talented pastry department at the Senator Restaurant in Toronto. Anne Hollyer is the genius behind the incredible cookies available daily in the diner.

2 1/2 cups (625ml)	all-purpose flour
1 tsp (5ml)	baking soda
1/2 tsp (2ml)	salt
1 cup (250ml)	brown sugar
1 cup (250ml)	granulated sugar
1 cup (250ml)	soft butter
3/4 cup (175ml)	peanut butter
3	eggs
1 tbsp (15ml)	vanilla
10 oz (300g)	milk chocolate chunks

Preheat oven to 350ºF (170ºC).

Sift together flour, baking soda, and salt. Cream together sugars, butter, and peanut butter until light and fluffy. Beat in eggs and vanilla.

Add dry ingredients to wet ingredients and stir together. Fold in chocolate chunks. Drop rounded tablespoons of dough 2 inches (5cm) apart on an ungreased cookie sheet.

Bake on the middle rack of the oven for 12 to 15 minutes or until golden.

Makes about 5 dozen cookies.

Plain and Peanutty Cookies

The peanut is not a nut at all — it is a legume. In the Southern United States, peanuts are called "goober peas" because the plant burrows its seeds (the peanuts) into the ground. For the same reason, peanuts are also known as "ground nuts."

1/2 cup (125ml)	soft butter
1/4 cup (50ml)	granulated sugar
1/4 cup (50ml)	brown sugar
1	egg
2 tsp (10ml)	lemon juice
1 tsp (5ml)	vanilla
1 1/4 cups (300ml)	all-purpose flour
1/2 tsp (2ml)	baking powder
1 cup (250ml)	chopped peanuts
1/2 cup (125ml)	chocolate-covered peanuts

Preheat oven to 375°F(190°C).

Cream together butter and sugars until light and fluffy. Beat in egg, then lemon juice and vanilla.

In a separate bowl, combine flour and baking powder. Stir flour mixture into creamed mixture in thirds. Fold in chopped peanuts.

Drop heaping teaspoons of dough 2 inches (5cm) apart on a greased cookie sheet. Press one chocolate covered peanut into the centre of each cookie.

Bake on the middle rack of the oven for 7 to 9 minutes or until golden. Transfer to cooling racks.

Makes about 4 dozen cookies.

Peanut Butter Chip Squares

I find squares simpler to make than cookies because they don't involve the same shaping. For more recipes for bars and squares, see "Everybody Loves a Square" (pp. 193–210).

1 1/2 cups (375ml)	all-purpose flour
1/2 cup (125ml)	packed golden sugar
1/4 tsp (1ml)	salt
1/2 cup (125ml)	cold butter, cut in cubes
2	eggs
1/2 cup (125ml)	whipping cream
1/2 cup (125ml)	cream cheese
1/3 cup (75ml)	granulated sugar
1 cup (250ml)	peanut butter chips
3/4 cup (175ml)	chocolate-covered peanuts

Preheat oven to 350ºF (180ºC).

In a medium bowl, combine flour, sugar, and salt. Rub in butter until the mixture is coarse and mealy. Press into an ungreased 8-inch (2L) square baking pan.

Bake on the middle rack of the oven for 15 minutes.

Meanwhile beat together egg, whipping cream, cream cheese, and sugar. Stir in peanut butter chips and chocolate covered peanuts. Pour over baked crust. Return pan to the oven for 25 minutes or until topping is set .

Let cool then cut into 2-inch (5cm) squares.

Makes 16 large squares.

Peanut Butter and Jam Sandwiches

This recipe was obviously designed to delight younger children.
Their favourite sandwich is transformed into a cookie!

1/2 cup (125ml)	soft butter
1/2 cup (125ml)	granulated sugar
1/2 cup (125ml)	packed golden sugar
2	eggs
1 tsp (5ml)	vanilla
1/2 cup (125ml)	peanut butter
1 1/2 cups (375ml)	all-purpose flour
1 tsp (5ml)	baking powder
2/3 cup (150ml)	jam (your choice)

Preheat oven to 350°F (180°C).

Cream together butter and sugars until light and fluffy. Beat in eggs, one at a time, then vanilla and peanut butter.

In a separate bowl, mix together flour and baking powder. Stir flour mixture into peanut butter mixture in thirds. Pour into an ungreased 13x9x2-inch (3.5L) pan.

Bake on the middle rack of the oven for 25 minutes or until golden.

Remove from oven and cut into 1 1/2-inch (4cm) squares. Cut each square in half horizontally. Spread jam over the bottom half and replace top half to make a sandwich.

Makes 45 squares.

Peanut Butter and Banana Cookies

This cookie was inspired by one of my favourite childhood lunch treats. My mother would spread peanut butter on a piece of bread, and cut a banana into eyes, a nose and a mouth for my banana face sandwich. These cookies should be fun for everyone who was treated to a similar indulgence.

1/2 cup (125ml)	soft butter
1/2 cup (125ml)	granulated sugar
1/2 cup (125ml)	packed brown sugar
1	egg
1/2 cup (125ml)	peanut butter
1	very ripe banana
2 1/4 cups (550ml)	all-purpose flour
3/4 tsp (4ml)	baking powder
1/4 tsp (1ml)	salt
1 cup (250ml)	banana chips

Cream together butter and sugars until light and fluffy. Beat in egg, then peanut butter and banana.

In a separate bowl, combine flour, baking powder, and salt. In a food processor, pulse 1/2 cup (125 ml) banana chips and stir into flour. Stir flour mixture into creamed butter in thirds. Refrigerate for 1 hour.

Preheat oven to 350ºF (180ºC).

Roll dough into 1-inch (2.5cm) balls and place 2 inches (5cm) apart on a parchment-lined cookie sheet. Press one banana chip into the centre of each cookie.

Bake on the middle rack of the oven for 10 minutes or until golden. Transfer to cooling rack.

Makes about 4 dozen cookies.

Peanut Butter and Banana Squares

Moving cookies or squares to a rack after baking allows air to circulate evenly around all sides, resulting in quick cooling. This is important because as long as the cookies or squares are hot, they will continue to cook.

1 cup (250ml)	all-purpose flour
1/2 cup (125ml)	cubed, cold butter
1/3 cup (75ml)	peanut butter
3	bananas
1/4 cup (50ml)	packed golden sugar
2 tbsp (25ml)	soft butter
1 tbsp (15ml)	lemon juice
3 oz (75g)	semi-sweet chocolate
2 tbsp (25ml)	chopped peanuts

Preheat oven to 350ºF (180ºC).

Rub cold butter into flour until coarse and mealy. Press into a greased 8-inch (2L) square baking pan. Bake on the middle rack of the oven for 10 minutes or until partially baked.

Spread peanut butter over warm crust. Cut bananas lengthwise into 3 long, thin slices. Combine golden sugar, butter, and lemon juice, then toss in bananas. Cover peanut butter layer with banana mixture.

Return to the oven and bake for 25 minutes or until golden. Transfer to cooling racks.

Melt chocolate in a double boiler or stainless steel bowl over hot (not boiling) water and drizzle over the surface of the cooled squares. Cover with peanuts and cut into 1 1/2-inch or 3-inch (4 or 8cm) squares.

Makes 3 dozen small or 9 large squares.

Peanut Butterscotch Cookies

*This uniquely simple recipe is ideally suited to hot summer days
when the idea of turning on the oven is unthinkable.*

1 cup (250ml)	butterscotch chips
1/2 cup (125 ml)	peanut butter
3 cups (750ml)	Rice Krispies™

Melt butterscotch chips over hot (not boiling) water. Stir in peanut butter.

Pour over Rice Krispies™ and stir to combine. Drop heaping teaspoonfuls on a waxed-paper-lined cookie sheet. Refrigerate for 2 hours or until set.

Makes about 5 dozen small cookies

A Taste of the West

Cookie Recipes from British Columbia, Alberta, Saskatchewan, and Manitoba

Throughout this book, and certainly in both the Christmas Cookie and the Great Canadian Cookie Contest chapters, there are examples of the generosity of western cooks. Whenever I send out a call for recipes, whether by contacting B&B's or by running a cooking contest, the response from the western provinces is terrific — and so is the food.

This isn't news. Hospitality is as characteristic of the West as the prairie wheat fields and has been since the days of the chuck wagon. Baking has been an honoured tradition since pioneer times when days of back-breaking labour were fuelled by bannock, homemade bread, and scones. Brown sugar and molasses, wild berries and sweet apples, cinnamon and cloves have been common ingredients in baked sweets since the turn of the last century.

Elli's B&B Biscotti

This recipe comes from Elli Stabile of Elli's B&B in Canmore, Alberta. Elli writes,
"We put biscotti in each room for the guests along with packaged cocoa, cappuccino,
and tea. I have recipes on cards for guests to take home and the biscotti is one
of the most requested recipes. Here is my basic recipe. The variations are endless —
just use your imagination to create different combinations."

1/2 cup (125ml)	sliced almonds
1/2 cup (125ml)	soft butter
1/2 cup (125ml)	sugar
2	eggs
1 tsp (5ml)	vanilla
1/4 tsp (1ml)	almond extract
2 tsp (10ml)	grated orange zest
2 1/4 (550ml)	cups all-purpose flour
1 1/2 tsp (7ml)	baking powder
1/2 tsp (2ml)	salt
1/8 tsp (.5ml)	nutmeg

Preheat oven to 350ºF (180ºC).

Toast almonds in oven for 8 to 10 minutes or until golden brown. Set aside to cool.

Cream butter and sugar until light and fluffy. Beat in eggs, vanilla, almond extract, and orange zest. In a separate bowl, combine flour, baking powder, salt and nutmeg. Add flour mixture to creamed butter in thirds, mixing until blended. Fold in almonds.

Divide dough in half and form into logs the length of your cookie sheet and 2 inches (5cm) in diameter. Place logs on a greased cookie sheet.

Bake on the middle rack of the oven for 25 minutes or until golden brown. Remove from oven and let cool for 10 minutes.

Place on cutting board and, using a serrated knife, slice each log diagonally at a 45-degree angle into 1/2 inch (1cm) pieces. Lay slices flat on baking sheet and return to oven.

Bake for 7 minutes, turn, and bake for an additional 7 minutes or until slightly dried and golden brown all over. Cool on rack, and store for up to one month in a container. Serve with cappuccino or coffee — dipping is encouraged!

Makes about 3 dozen cookies.

Variations

Double Chocolate Biscotti: Add 1/3 cup (75 ml) cocoa and 1 cup (250ml) chocolate chips to dry ingredients. Omit nutmeg.

Gianduia Biscotti: Add 1/3 cup (125ml) hazelnuts with the almonds. Add 5 oz (150g) melted unsweetened chocolate. Substitute 1/4 cup (50ml) brown sugar for 1/4 cup (50ml) granulated sugar. Add 1 tbsp Frangelico or double-strength coffee to creamed butter. Omit almond extract and grated orange zest.

Betty's Oatmeal Cookies

The next three recipes come from Andrea Gailus at the Cougar Canyon B&B in Canmore, Alberta. Andrea writes, "In my recipe box, the cards that have the most stains stand out as favourites. I'm sending you two of those plus one new arrival that is a result of my husband's recent diagnosis of diabetes. The recipe for oatmeal cookies comes from Betty Brandon, a long time neighbour and family friend in Calgary, who lovingly cared for our four young children when we went on weekend getaways."

1/2 cup (125ml)	soft butter
1/2 cup (125ml)	brown sugar
1/4 cup (50ml)	granulated sugar
1	egg
1 tsp (5ml)	vanilla
2/3 cup (150ml)	all-purpose flour
1/2 tsp (2ml)	baking soda
1/2 tsp (2ml)	salt
1 cup (250ml)	quick-cooking oats
1 cup (250ml)	chocolate chips
1/2 cup (125ml)	chopped nuts
1/2 cup (125ml)	raisins

Preheat oven to 350ºF (180ºC).

Cream together butter and sugars until light and fluffy. Beat in egg and vanilla.

Combine flour, baking soda, and salt. Stir in oatmeal, chocolate chips, nuts, and raisins. Stir dry ingredients into wet ingredients.

Roll dough into 1-inch (2.5cm) balls and place on a greased cookie sheet.

Bake in the middle rack of the oven for 8 to 10 minutes or until golden.

Makes about 2 dozen cookies.

Low-fat Variation: Substitute 1/2 cup (125ml) applesauce for the butter, 3/4 cup (175 ml) Splenda for the sugars, and whole wheat flour for the all-purpose flour.

Snicker Doodles

Andrea Gailus at the Cougar Canyon B&B in Canmore, Alberta, writes,
"This recipe came from Steve Barkey's mom about twenty years ago.
Our sons played with Steve and ate all her Snicker Doodles so she sent the
recipe home with them for me to make some."

1 cup (250ml)	shortening
1 1/2 cups (375ml)	sugar
2	eggs
2 3/4 cups (675ml)	flour
1 tsp (5ml)	cream of tartar
1 tsp (5ml)	baking soda
1/4 tsp (1ml)	salt
2 tbsp (25ml)	sugar (for dusting)
2 tsp (10ml)	cinnamon (for dusting)

Preheat oven to 400ºF (200ºC).

Cream together shortening and sugar. Beat in eggs. In another bowl, combine flour, cream of tartar, baking soda, and salt. Stir dry ingredients into wet ingredients.

Form dough into 1-inch (2.5cm) balls. Combine sugar and cinnamon and roll balls in mixture to cover. Place balls on a lightly-greased cookie sheet.

Bake on the middle rack of the oven for 8 to 10 minutes or until edges are golden.

Makes about 4 dozen cookies.

Mocha Oatmeal Cookies

Here's one more recipe from Andrea Gailus, of Canmore, Alberta. "I bake these cookies for my husband, who has diabetes. When you replace the oil with apple sauce and the sugar with Splenda they become low in fat and sugar."

2 cups (500ml)	all-purpose flour
1 cup (250ml)	cocoa powder
2 cups (500ml)	rolled oats
1 cup (250ml)	bran
1 tsp (5ml)	baking soda
1/2 tsp (2ml)	salt
1/2 cup (125ml)	canola oil OR apple sauce
1 cup (250ml)	brown sugar OR Splenda
1 cup (250ml)	granulated sugar OR Splenda
2	large eggs
1/4 cup (50ml)	strong coffee, cooled
1/2 cup (125ml)	coffee-flavoured yogurt
2 tsp (10ml)	vanilla

Preheat oven to 350ºF (180ºC).

Combine flour, cocoa, oats, bran, baking soda, and salt, and set aside. In a second bowl, beat oil and sugars together until smooth. Beat in eggs, coffee, yogurt, and vanilla.

Blend wet ingredients into dry ingredients until well combined, and let sit for 10 minutes to allow liquid to absorb. Drop tablespoons of dough on a lightly-greased or parchment-lined cookie sheet.

Bake on middle rack of oven for 8 to 10 minutes or until puffy. Transfer to cooling racks.

Makes about 5 dozen cookies.

Harvest Granola Cookies

The wheat fields of the prairies have long been an intrinsic part of our Canadian identity. Since the early days of settlement, hard flour has been used for most baking in the western provinces.

1/2 cup (125ml)	soft butter
1 cup (250ml)	sugar
1	egg
1 tsp (5ml)	vanilla
1/4 cup (50ml)	sour cream
1 1/2 cups (375ml)	all-purpose flour
1/2 tsp (2ml)	baking powder
1/2 tsp (2ml)	baking soda
1 cup (250ml)	granola
1/2 cup (125ml)	harvest dried fruit mix

Preheat oven to 350ºF (180ºC).

Cream together butter and sugar until light and fluffy. Beat in egg, then vanilla and sour cream.

Mix together flour, baking powder, and baking soda. In a food processor, pulse granola and dried fruit until the mixture resembles coarse crumbs. Stir into flour mixture. Stir flour mixture into creamed butter in thirds. Drop heaping teaspoons of dough 2 inches (5cm) apart on a greased cookie sheet.

Bake on the middle rack of the oven for 10 to 12 minutes or until golden. Transfer to cooling racks.

Makes about 3 dozen cookies.

Saskatoon-Berry Squares

*This recipe was inspired by the Saskatoon-Berry Pie introduced to me
by Murray McMillan of the Vancouver Sun. Of course, in Ontario,
I have to resort to good old blueberries to make these squares.*

1 1/2 cups (375ml)	all-purpose flour
1/4 cup (50ml)	brown sugar
1 tsp (5ml)	cinnamon
1/4 tsp (2ml)	ground ginger
1/4 tsp (2ml)	salt
1 1/2 cups (375ml)	rolled oats
1 cup (250ml)	cold butter, cut in cubes
2	eggs, beaten

FILLING

4 cups (1L)	Saskatoon berries OR blueberries
1/4 cup (50ml)	sugar
2 tbsp (25ml)	sifted all-purpose flour
1/2 tsp (2ml)	salt
1 tbsp (15ml)	soft butter
1 tbsp (15ml)	lemon juice

Preheat oven to 375°F (190°C).

Combine flour, sugar, cinnamon, ginger and salt. Stir in oats. Rub in butter until mixture has a coarse, mealy texture. Stir in eggs. Press three quarters of dough into a 8-inch (2L) square pan. Refrigerate the remaining dough.

Bake crust in middle rack of oven for 15 minutes. Set aside to cool.

Pick, wash, and drain berries and toss with sugar, flour, lemon juice, and salt. Spread berries over crust and dot with butter. Top with remaining dough.

Bake for 25 minutes or until top is golden. Let cool to set before cutting into 2-inch (5cm) squares.

Makes 16 squares.

Raisin Almond Cookies

In the old days of the west, cowboys on cattle drives would be fed by an ornery cook from his chuck wagon. Since there was no refrigeration, they relied heavily on dried fruit for desserts. Raisins were baked into pies and boiled into puddings to add a hint of sweetness at the end of a hard day.

1/4 cup (50ml)	shortening
1/2 cup (125ml)	sugar
1	egg
1 tsp (5ml)	lemon juice
1/2 cup (125ml)	whipping cream
1 1/2 cups (375ml)	all-purpose flour
1 tsp (5ml)	baking powder
1/4 tsp (2ml)	salt
2 cups (500ml)	plumped raisins
24	chocolate-covered almonds

Preheat oven to 375ºF (180ºC).

Cream together shortening and sugar. Beat in egg, lemon juice and then cream.

In a separate bowl, combine flour, baking powder and salt. Stir in raisins. Stir flour mixture into creamed mixture in thirds.

Drop heaping teaspoons of dough 2 inches (5cm) apart on a greased cookie sheet. Gently press one chocolate-covered almond into the centre of each cookie.

Bake on the middle rack of the oven for 10 to 12 minutes. Transfer to cooling racks.

Makes about 3 dozen cookies.

Forest Ranger Cookies

Dora Miner of Millet, Alberta, has a marvelous website featuring food, recipes and other internet goodies. If you like her cookies — and I'm sure you will — visit her at www.telusplanet.net/public/minerda/doras.htm and check out some of her other food stylings.

1 cup (250ml)	soft butter
1 cup (250ml)	sugar
2	eggs
1 tsp (5ml)	vanilla
2 cups (500ml)	all-purpose flour
1 tsp (5ml)	baking soda
1 tsp (5ml)	baking powder
1 tsp (5ml)	salt
2 cups (500ml)	oatmeal
2 cups (500ml)	coconut
2 cups (500ml)	Rice Krispies™

Preheat oven to 350ºF (180ºC).

Cream together butter and sugar until light and fluffy. Beat in eggs, one at a time, then vanilla. In a separate bowl, mix flour with baking soda, baking powder, and salt. Stir in oatmeal, coconut, and Rice Krispies.™

Stir flour mixture into creamed mixture in thirds. Roll dough into 1 1/2 inch (4cm) balls, place 3 inches (8cm) apart on a parchment-lined cookie sheet, and flatten slightly with a fork.

Bake for 10 to 15 minutes or until golden. Transfer to cooling racks.

Makes about 3 dozen cookies.

Central Canadian Cookies

Recipes from Ontario and Quebec

There are certain similarities in cookie recipes from across Canada —
the classics are popular and there is a pronounced preference for
drop cookies. Although Canadian regional cuisine certainly exists,
for the most part cookies seem to be a great equalizer. Still, for me,
this chapter is special for two reasons.

First of all, it contains recipes from Quebec, the centre of our
French heritage. Some of Canada's best culinary traditions originate
in central Canada and it is always exciting to explore *la cuisine régionale
au Quebec*. Quebec is also close to my heart, because my mother's family
was French Canadian, as was André Théberge, the wonderful chef
with whom I apprenticed. Second, I am a product of Ontario. I was born in
Windsor, I worked for twenty years in the Toronto restaurant industry,
I spent a few years enjoying the fresh foods of Waterloo County, and
now I am raising a family in a small town several hours north of Toronto.
I have enjoyed the produce and cuisine of this province all my life
and it's always a pleasure to share them.

Coconut Cream Pie Cookies

This recipe was inspired by the mile-high cream pies I lusted after as a child. The Tunnel Barbecue in my home town of Windsor, Ontario, made the most spectacular pies, and my sister and I would often cajole our father into taking us there. If you like your whipped cream sweet, incorporate 1 tbsp (15ml) of sugar while beating the cream

1/2 cup (125ml)	soft butter
1 cup (250ml)	packed golden sugar
1	egg
1 tsp (5ml)	vanilla
1 1/2 cups (375ml)	all-purpose flour
1/2 tsp (2ml)	baking soda
3/4 cup (175ml)	unsweetened coconut
1/3 cup (75ml)	whipping cream
2 tbsp (25ml)	toasted coconut

Cream together butter and sugar until light and fluffy. Beat in egg and vanilla.

In a separate bowl, mix together flour and baking soda. Stir flour mixture into creamed mixture in thirds. Fold in coconut. Refrigerate for 1 hour.

Preheat oven to 350ºF (180ºC).

Roll dough into 1-inch (2.5cm) balls and place 2 inches (5cm) apart on an ungreased cookie sheet.

Bake on the middle rack of the oven for 8 to 10 minutes or until golden. Transfer to cooling racks.

Before serving, whip cream until peaks form, spoon a dollop of fresh cream on the centre of each cookie, and top with a pinch of toasted coconut.

Makes about 3 dozen cookies.

Hazelnut Cookies

Jessy van Remortel is from the Netherlands but she has lived in Toronto for the past forty years. This recipe was given to her by the wife of the doctor who delivered Jessy's daughter Monique. Monique is now a lawyer and continues to bake these cookies for their simplicity.

7 oz (200g)	hazelnuts, finely ground
4 oz (100g)	white granulated sugar
2	egg whites
1 tsp (5ml)	almond extract

Preheat oven to 325°F (160°C).

In a food processor, combine hazelnuts, sugar, egg whites, and almond extract, and blend to a paste. Drop teaspoons of batter on a greased cookie sheet. Do not flatten. Garnish each cookie with a slivered almond.

Bake on the middle rack of the oven for 12 to 15 minutes or until crispy at the edges. Transfer to cooling racks.

Makes about 2 dozen cookies.

Lemon Ginger Tuiles

These tuiles are based on a recipe I made while working at the Provence Restaurant in Toronto's Cabbagetown. Once the method is mastered, these cookies are remarkably simple to make. It is important to shape the tuiles quickly while they are warm. If they become too brittle to work, pop them back in the oven for a moment to soften.

1/4 cup (50ml)	soft butter
1/2 cup (125ml)	sugar
1 tbsp (15ml)	minced, candied lemon zest
1/2 tsp (2ml)	vanilla
2	egg whites
1/2 cup (125ml)	all-purpose flour
1 tsp (5ml)	ground ginger

Preheat oven to 350ºF (180ºC).

Beat together butter, sugar, lemon zest, and vanilla until light and fluffy. Beat in egg whites. The mixture will appear curdled. Combine flour and ginger and fold into butter mixture.

Line a cookie sheet with buttered parchment paper. Drop one tablespoon of batter on the sheet and spread it into a circle 4 to 5 inches (10 to 12cm) in diameter. Repeat until cookie sheet is full.

Bake in middle rack of oven. After 5 minutes, turn the cookies over, and bake for an additional 3 minutes or until edges are golden brown.

Remove from oven and immediately drape cookies over small cups to give them a bowl shape. Handle carefully. Serve dusted with icing sugar or filled with fresh whipped cream.

Makes 12 cookies.

Rich Pecan Squares

This recipe comes from Elizabeth Baird's Classic Canadian Cooking. Pecan squares are a definitely a classic and deservedly so — it's impossible to deny their rich charms. And speaking of charming, Elizabeth is truly marvelous in her support and encouragement of Canadian cuisine and those who cook and write about it.

1/3 cup (75ml)	soft butter
1 1/2 cups (375ml)	firmly packed brown sugar
1	egg, separated
1 1/4 tsp (6ml)	vanilla
3/4 cup (175ml)	sifted all-purpose flour
1 tsp (5ml)	baking powder
1/2 tsp (2ml)	salt
3/4 cup (175ml)	chopped pecans

Preheat oven to 325ºF (160ºC).

Cream the butter until light and fluffy. Gradually beat in 1 cup (250ml) of brown sugar, the yolk of the egg, and 1 tsp (5ml) of vanilla, and continue beating to make a smooth creamy batter.

Sift together flour, baking powder, and salt. Stir into the creamed mixture, along with 1/2 cup (125ml) of chopped pecans.

Spoon batter evenly into a greased 11x7-inch (2L) cake tin. Beat egg white until stiff but not dry. Beat in the remaining 1/2 cup (125ml) sugar and 1/4 tsp (1ml) vanilla. Spread this topping over the batter and sprinkle with the remaining 1/4 cup (50ml) chopped pecans.

Bake for 35 to 40 minutes or until the top is lightly browned and the mixture has pulled away from the sides.

Makes 2 dozen squares.

Cocoa Quickies

This recipe comes from my friend, Brenda Kuntz, of Waterloo, Ontario, who writes.
"I found this recipe in the archives. It was the first cookie my mother and I ever made
together, thirty years ago. It's simple and there is no baking involved."

1 1/2 (375ml)	cups rolled oats
1/4 cup (50ml)	shredded coconut
1/4 cup (50ml)	chopped nuts
2 tbsp (25ml)	cocoa
1/4 cup (50ml)	soft butter
1/2 cup (125ml)	granulated sugar
1/4 cup (50ml)	brown sugar
1/4 cup (50ml)	cream
1 tsp (5ml)	vanilla

In a large bowl, mix together oats, coconut, nuts, and cocoa.

In a medium saucepan over medium heat, melt butter. Stir in sugars, cream, and vanilla, and heat for one minute.

Pour wet mixture over dry ingredients and stir until combined. Drop heaping teaspoons of batter on a waxed-paper-lined cookie sheet. Refrigerate for 2 hours or until set.

Store cookies in a tin with waxed paper between the layers.

Makes about 3 dozen small cookies.

Sensational Turtle Brownies

Here's a page from one of Rose Murray's wonderful books —
Rose Murray's Comfortable Kitchen Cookbook. These marvelous brownies
have become a Canadian standard and I often see them imitated.

1 cup (250ml)	butter, in pieces
4 oz (125g)	unsweetened chocolate, coarsely chopped
1 3/4 cups (425ml)	granulated sugar
4	eggs, well beaten
1 tsp (5ml)	vanilla
1 1/4 cups (300ml)	all purpose flour
1/2 tsp (2ml)	salt

TOPPING

1/2 cup (125ml)	whipping cream
1/2 cup (125ml)	packed brown sugar
1/4 cup (50ml)	soft butter
1 1/2 cups (375ml)	pecan halves
1 cup (250ml)	chocolate chips

Preheat oven to 400ºF (200ºC).

In top of double boiler over simmering water, melt butter and chocolate. Remove from heat and stir in sugar until well combined. Stir in eggs and vanilla.

Gradually add flour and salt, stirring well after each addition. Pour into greased 13x9-inch (3.5L) baking pan.

Bake for 10 minutes. (The batter will not be totally cooked but will be set enough to add topping.)

Meanwhile, combine cream, brown sugar, and butter in a saucepan. Bring to a boil and boil for 2 minutes. Sprinkle partially-baked base with pecans and drizzle evenly with caramel syrup.

Bake for an additional 8 to 10 minutes or until golden but not browned.

Remove from oven. Sprinkle with chocolate chips. Let the chocolate melt slightly for 1 to 2 minutes, then swirl with knife so that some caramel and nuts show through. Cool on rack and cut into squares.

Makes 16 squares.

Cranberry Granola Cookies

Nothing signals autumn in Canada quite like cranberries. From the unbeatable berries of Maseau, Quebec to the wild berries grown on vines in the bogs of Ontario, this tart, juicy fruit is used in baking, served with duck, and of course, stewed for sauce at Thanksgiving.

1 cup (250ml)	soft butter
1 1/3 cups (325ml)	sugar
2	eggs
1 tsp (5ml)	vanilla
1 3/4 cups (425ml)	all-purpose flour
1 cup (250ml)	granola
1 tsp (5ml)	baking soda
1/4 tsp (1ml)	salt (omit if granola contains salt)
1 cup (250ml)	dried cranberries

Preheat oven to 350ºF (180ºC).

Cream together butter and sugar until light and fluffy. Beat in eggs, one at a time, then vanilla.

Mix together flour, granola, baking soda, and salt. Stir flour mixture into creamed butter in thirds. Fold in cranberries.

Drop heaping tablespoons of dough 2 inches (5cm) apart on a greased baking sheet.

Bake on the middle rack of the oven for 8 to 10 minutes or until edges are browned. Transfer to cooling racks.

Makes about 3 dozen cookies.

Lemon Sunflower Cookies

Sunflowers were growing on this continent long before the first Europeans set foot on our shores. This majestic plant thrives in the long, hot days of summer as it follows the sun on its daily course. Is it any wonder that the seeds taste sun-kissed?

1/2 cup (125ml)	soft butter
1 cup (250ml)	packed golden sugar
1	egg
1 tsp (5ml)	vanilla
1 1/2 cups (375ml)	all-purpose flour
1/2 tsp (2ml)	baking soda
1 tbsp (15ml)	finely grated lemon zest
1/2 cup (125ml)	honey-roasted sunflower seeds

Cream together butter and sugar until light and fluffy. Beat in egg and vanilla.

Mix together flour, baking soda, and lemon zest. Stir flour mixture into creamed butter in thirds. Fold in sunflower seeds. Refrigerate for 1 hour.

Preheat oven to 350°F (180°C).

Roll dough into 1-inch (2.5cm) balls and place 2 inches (5cm) apart on an ungreased cookie sheet. Flatten each ball with the bottom of a glass dipped in sugar.

Bake on the middle rack of the oven for 8 to 10 minutes or until golden. Transfer to cooling racks.

Makes about 3 dozen cookies.

Cranberry Apple-Butter Cookies

Without a doubt, the best thing about living in Waterloo County is the food.
A favourite pastime of mine was to visit the local farms and buy their
remarkable goods. From fresh eggs to apple butter made by Mennonites, there
is always something homemade or farm-raised in my cupboard.

1 cup (250ml)	soft butter
3/4 cup (175ml)	granulated sugar
3/4 cup (175ml)	firmly packed brown sugar
1/2 cup (125ml)	apple butter
1	egg
1 2/3 cups (400ml)	all-purpose flour
1 tsp (5ml)	baking soda
1/2 tsp (2ml)	salt
2 cups (500ml)	rolled oats
2 cups (500ml)	sweetened, dried cranberries

Preheat oven to 375°F (190°C).

Cream together butter and sugars until light and fluffy. Beat in apple butter and egg.

Mix together flour, baking soda, and salt. Add oats. Stir flour mixture into creamed butter in thirds. Fold in cranberries.

Drop heaping tablespoons of dough 3 inches (8cm) apart on a parchment-lined cookie sheet.

Bake on the middle rack of the oven for 12 to 14 minutes or until golden. Transfer to cooling racks.

Makes about 4 dozen cookies.

Buttered Almond Crisps

Almonds may be a product of the Mediterranean, but they have found a welcome place in Canada's pantries. Their nutritional value is extremely high — they contribute calcium, folic acid, magnesium, potassium, riboflavin, and vitamin E to these cookies. Encourage guests to have more than one, for health's sake.

1/2 cup (125ml)	soft butter
1 cup (250ml)	firmly packed brown sugar
1	egg
1 tsp (5ml)	vanilla
1 tsp (5ml)	almond extract
1 1/2 cups (375ml)	all-purpose flour
1/2 tsp (2ml)	baking soda
1 cup (250ml)	buttered almonds

Cream together butter and sugar until smooth. Beat in egg, then vanilla and almond extract.

Mix together flour and baking soda. In a food processor, pulse 1/2 cup (125ml) of almonds until fine. Mix ground almonds into flour. Stir flour mixture into creamed butter in thirds. Refrigerate for 1 hour.

Preheat oven to 375ºF (190ºC).

Roll dough into 1-inch (2.5cm) balls and place 2 inches (5cm) apart on a parchment-lined cookie sheet. Flatten each ball slightly with the bottom of a glass dipped in sugar. Press one whole buttered almond in the centre of each cookie.

Bake on the middle rack of the oven for 6 to 10 minutes or until the edges are golden. Transfer to cooling rack.

Makes about 4 dozen cookies.

Mum Ogilvie's Lacy Cookies

This recipe was contributed by Dawn Murdoch of Addison's Private Garden Suites and Guest Cottage in Niagara-on-the-Lake. She can be reached at ⟨addisons@niagara.com⟩. Dawn writes, "Mum Ogilvie was born in 1907, at a time when women expressed love for their family by the extras they baked. She really knew how to love as well as bake, and I miss her." Gram's hint: This recipe works best if you can fill more than one cookie tray at a time.

2 cups (500ml)	firmly packed brown sugar
3 tbsp (50ml)	all-purpose flour
1 tsp (5ml)	salt
3 cups (370ml)	quick-cooking oats
1/2 lb (250g)	butter, melted
1	egg, beaten
1 tsp (5ml)	vanilla

Preheat oven to 375ºF (190ºC).

Mix together sugar, flour, and salt. Stir in oats. Stir in butter then egg and vanilla.

Drop heaping teaspoons of dough 3 inches (8cm) apart on a slightly-greased cookie sheet. Flatten with a fork.

Bake on the middle rack of the oven. Turn the cookie sheet after 1 1/2 minutes, and bake for 3 to 5 minutes or until golden brown. Cool on cookie sheet for 2 minutes then transfer to cooling rack.

Makes about 5 dozen cookies.

Coffee Hazelnut Cookies

This recipe comes from Sasha Chapman, the senior food editor for President's Choice Magazine. Sasha writes. "Here are my favourite cookies. The key to success when making these cookies is to grind the hazelnuts as finely as possible without turning them into a paste."

3 tbsp (50ml)	granulated sugar
1 cup (250ml)	toasted hazelnuts
1/2 cup (125ml)	soft butter
2 tsp (10ml)	instant coffee
1 cup (250ml)	all-purpose flour
1 oz (25g)	grated semi-sweet chocolate
18	large chocolate chips
1/4 cup (50ml)	ganache OR chocolate-hazelnut spread
2 tbsp (25ml)	icing sugar

Preheat oven to 325ºF (160ºC).

In a food processor, grind hazelnuts with sugar. Transfer to a bowl and cream with butter until light and fluffy. Dissolve coffee in 1 tbsp (15ml) water and beat into creamed mixture. Stir in flour and grated chocolate in thirds.

Roll dough into 1/2-inch (4cm) balls and place on a parchment-lined cookie sheet. Flatten each ball slightly with the back of a spoon. Press one chocolate chip into half of the cookies

Bake on the middle rack of the oven for 12 to 15 minutes or until firm. (The cookies will not change in appearance during baking.) Transfer to cooling racks.

When cool, spread ganache on plain cookies and cover with a chocolate-topped cookie. Sift icing sugar over top.

Makes about 3 dozen cookies.

Chow Chow Cookies

These cookies were created by Anna Hariton at her father's bakery in Guelph, Ontario. I love to see different variations of no-bake cookies because they are simple and pleasant to make, even on a sweltering summer day.

1 cup (250ml)	pretzels
1 cup (250ml)	Rice Krispies™
1 cup (250ml)	Corn Chex OR Wheat Chex
1 cup (250ml)	peanuts
1 cup (250ml)	M&M's™
12 oz (375g)	white chocolate squares
1/2 cup (125ml)	icing sugar
Pinch	of salt

Combine pretzels, Rice Krispies,™ Chex, peanuts, and candies.

Melt chocolate in a double boiler or stainless steel bowl over hot (not boiling) water. Stir in icing sugar and salt. Fold in the dry ingredients.

Drop by small handfuls onto a parchment-lined cookie sheet. Place in refrigerator and chill for 2 hours or until set.

Makes about 2 dozen cookies.

Biscuits au sirop d'érable (Maple Cookies)

This recipe comes from Julian Armstrong's book, A Taste of Quebec.
Pauline Jacques runs the cooking school Les Ateliers de Pauline at Granby, Quebec.
She remembers both her mother and grandmother making these cookies when she
was growing up, and the maple syrup came from her grandfather's maple woods in
South Stukeley. This family recipe is based on one from a treasured cookbook,
Cuisineière de la révérende Mère Caron, published in 1908 by the director of Quebec's
first domestic science school run by the Ursulines at Roberval on Lac St-Jean.

1 cup (250ml)	soft butter
1 cup (250ml)	brown sugar
2	eggs, beaten
1/3 cup (75ml)	maple syrup
1 tsp (5ml)	vanilla
3 1/2 cups (875ml)	pastry flour
2 tsp (10ml)	baking powder
1/2 tsp (2ml)	salt

In a large bowl, cream butter with brown sugar until fluffy. Beat in eggs, maple syrup, and vanilla until well combined. In a separate bowl, sift together 3 cups (750ml) of flour, baking powder, and salt.

Beat dry ingredients into creamed mixture. Slowly add remaining flour until the dough comes away from the sides of the bowl and forms a ball. Cover dough and refrigerate for 2 hours or until firm.

Preheat oven to 350ºF (180ºC).

On a lightly-floured surface, roll out dough thinly and cut into desired shapes.

Bake on lightly-greased baking sheets for 8 to 10 minutes or until edges are lightly browned and crisp. Place on racks to cool.

Makes 5 to 6 dozen cookies, depending on the size.

Gallettes à la mélasse (Molasses Cookies)

Molasses is a secondary product of sugar production. When sugar cane is juiced, the sugar to be refined is extracted from the liquid — the remaining dark syrup is molasses. There have been many periods in our history when molasses was more available, or less expensive, than sugar, and much of our country-style baking reflects this fact.

2 cups (500ml)	all-purpose flour
1 tsp (5ml)	baking soda
1 tsp (5ml)	ground ginger
1 tsp (5ml)	cinnamon
1/2 tsp (2ml)	ground cloves
1/2 tsp (2ml)	freshly grated nutmeg
1/2 tsp (2ml)	salt
1/2 cup (125ml)	molasses
1/3 cup (75ml)	soft butter
1/2 cup (125ml)	brown sugar
1/3 cup (75ml)	milk
1 tsp (5ml)	vanilla

Sift together flour, baking soda, ginger, cinnamon, cloves, nutmeg, and salt.

In a medium pot over low heat, gently warm the molasses and butter. Stir in sugar, milk, and vanilla. Slowly stir in flour mixture until combined. Transfer to a bowl, cover with plastic wrap or cloth, and refrigerate for 2 hours.

Preheat oven to 375ºF (190ºC).

Divide dough into four portions and work with one portion at a time. Roll out dough on a well-floured surface to 1/4 inch (5mm) thickness. Dust with extra flour. Cut into rounds or shapes as desired.

Bake for 7 to 10 minutes (depending on size) or until edges are darkened.

Makes about 4 dozen galettes.

Galettes au sirop (Syrup Soft Cookies)

Cookbook author Micheline Mongrain writes "Here is the recipe I suggest for a special cookie from Quebec. These are softer than regular cookies and denser than cakes. I suggest baking in the middle of the oven to prevent over-browning the bottom of the galette. This recipe is published in my cookbook Traditional Quebec Cooking that we still sell all over Canada. It was first published in 1995. These galettes are a favourite in the Saguenay Lac St-Jean area. The taste is similar to Galettes à la mélasse but the texture is slightly different."

1/2 cup (125ml)	shortening
3/4 cup (190ml)	sugar
2	eggs
3/4 cup (190ml)	molasses
1/2 cup (125ml)	strong coffee
3 1/4 cups (800ml)	all-purpose flour
1/2 tsp (2ml)	salt
1 tbsp (15ml)	baking soda

In a large bowl cream shortening. Add sugar and eggs and beat well. Add molasses, then coffee.

Combine flour, salt, and baking soda, and add to the batter. Set batter aside for half an hour.

Preheat oven to 375°F (190°C).

On a generously-floured surface, roll out dough to a thickness of 1/3 inch (1cm) Sprinkle top of dough with flour, then roll out. Cut out 3-inch (8cm) rounds with a pastry cutter, and place 2 inches (5cm) apart on a lightly-greased cookie sheet.

Bake for 15 minutes. Cool on wire rack and store in an airtight container.

Makes 2 dozen galettes.

Maple Walnut Cookies

Yes, there is much more to Canadian cuisine than maple syrup but it's one of our best home-grown products and it does add a distinctive taste to these cookies.

1 cup (250ml)	soft butter
1 cup (250ml)	firmly packed brown sugar
1	egg
1/2 cup (125ml)	maple syrup
2 cups (500ml)	all-purpose flour
1 cup (250ml)	whole wheat flour
1 tsp (5ml)	baking soda
1 tsp (5ml)	cinnamon
1/4 tsp (1ml)	salt
1 cup (250ml)	chopped walnuts
1 cup (250ml)	walnut halves

Preheat oven to 350ºF (180ºC).

Cream together butter and sugar until light and fluffy. Beat in egg, then maple syrup.

In a separate bowl, stir together flours, baking soda, cinnamon, and salt. Stir flour mixture into creamed butter in thirds. Fold in chopped walnuts.

Drop heaping tablespoons of batter 2 inches (5cm) apart on a parchment-lined cookie sheet. Press a walnut half into each cookie.

Bake on the middle rack of the oven for 10 to 12 minutes or until golden. Transfer to cooling racks.

Makes about 3 dozen cookies.

Almond Sablés

Sablés, or sand cookies, have a marvelous dry texture and come in a variety of flavours. This almond version can be dressed with a coating of melted chocolate.

3/4 cup (175ml)	soft butter
3/4 cup (175ml)	powdered sugar
1	egg yolk
1 tsp (5ml)	vanilla
1 1/4 cups (300ml)	all-purpose flour
1/2 cup (125ml)	ground almonds
1/3 cup (75ml)	slivered almonds

Cream together butter and sugar until light and fluffy. Beat in egg yolk and vanilla.

In a separate bowl, combine flour and ground almonds. Stir flour mixture into creamed mixture in thirds. Refrigerate for 2 hours.

Preheat oven to 350ºF (180ºC).

Between two sheets of waxed paper, roll dough out to 1/4 inch (5mm) thickness. Refrigerate for 2 hours or until firm. Cut out 2-inch (5cm) rounds and place on a parchment-lined cookie sheet. Press 3 slivered almonds into each round in a fan shape.

Bake on the middle rack of the oven for 10 minutes or until edges are browned. Transfer to cooling racks.

Makes about 2 dozen cookies.

Madeleines

This elegant French cookie also appeared in Nice Timing, the book based on my columns from President's Choice Magazine. A madeleine pan, with its lovely scalloped design, is ideal, but if you don't have one, a mini-muffin tin will do.

1/4 cup (50ml)	soft butter
1/3 cup (75ml)	sugar
2	eggs, room temperature
1/2 tsp (2ml)	vanilla
1 tbsp (15ml)	brandy (optional)
2/3 cup (150ml)	flour
1/2 tsp (2ml)	baking powder
Pinch	salt
1 tbsp (15ml)	berry jam
1 tbsp (15ml)	icing sugar

Preheat oven to 425ºF (220ºC).

Cream together butter and sugar until light and fluffy. Beat in eggs, vanilla, and 2 tsp (10ml) brandy, if using.

In a separate bowl, stir together flour, baking powder, and salt. Fold into wet ingredients in thirds. Spoon batter into greased madeleine pans.

Bake in the middle rack of the oven for 8 minutes or until they spring back to the touch. Set aside to cool. Before serving, combine jam and remaining tsp (5ml) brandy and drizzle over top.

Makes 10 madeleines.

An Eastern Experience

Cookie Recipes from New Brunswick, Nova Scotia, Prince Edward Island, and Newfoundland

Atlantic Canada is as beautiful as any place on earth. Sandy beaches, roaring ocean, lush farmland, and craggy coasts, such as the Cabot Trail on Cape Breton, abound. The economy in the region has been a constant challenge to its people, and yet east coasters are known across the country for their warm and sunny disposition.

The culinary traditions of this region have their roots in both Acadian and British culture, but have been adapted to accommodate the foods of the coast. Despite troubles with the fisheries, the sea still provides fresh, delicious bounty, and the countryside yields fiddleheads, berries, rhubarb, and of course, potatoes. As for cookies, they are similar to those baked all across the country: molasses cookies, sugar cookies, and lemon squares all appear in this chapter. There are, however, two uniquely East Coast recipes that contain potato flour.

Nutty Squares

These cookies come to us courtesy of Rosemary Evans at the Old Orchard Bed and Breakfast in Prince Edward Island. She writes, "Here are two favourites of my family and also of our many guests. The first is a rich nutty cookie that is almost like candy."

1	egg
1 cup (250ml)	brown sugar
1/2 tsp (2ml)	vanilla
1/2 cup (125ml)	sifted all-purpose flour
1/2 tsp (2ml)	salt
1/8 tsp (.5ml)	baking soda
1 cup (250ml)	walnuts
2 tbsp (25ml)	confectioner's sugar

Preheat oven to 325°F (160°C).

Beat egg until foamy. Beat in brown sugar and vanilla.

Sift together flour, salt, and baking soda, and stir into egg mixture. Mix in walnuts and stir to combine. Spread dough in a well-greased 8-inch (2L) square baking pan.

Bake for 35 minutes or until the top has developed a dull crust.

Cut into 2-inch (5cm) squares while still warm. Cool and remove from pan. Sprinkle top with icing sugar.

Makes 16 squares.

Luscious Lemon Bars

Rosemary Evans writes, "This lemon bar is delicious, tart and very rich. Our B&B guests enjoy these wonderful treats at any time, but especially on warm, summer evenings."

1 cup (250ml)	soft butter
2/3 cup (150ml)	confectioners' sugar
1 tsp (5ml)	vanilla
2 cups (500ml)	all-purpose flour
4	eggs
2 cups (500ml)	granulated sugar
Grated rind	of one lemon
6 tbsp (100ml)	lemon juice

Preheat oven to 350ºF (180ºC).

Cream butter, 1/2 cup (125ml) confectioners' sugar, and vanilla until light and fluffy. Mix in flour until well-blended. Spread evenly into a well-buttered 13x9-inch (3.5L) baking pan.

Bake for 20 minutes or until firm.

Meanwhile, stir (do not beat) eggs, granulated sugar, lemon rind, and lemon juice together until combined. Pour egg mixture over baked layer. Return to the oven for 18 to 22 minutes or until topping is set and lightly browned.

While still warm, sift additional confectioners' sugar over top to cover generously. Cut into 1x2 1/2-inch (2.5x6cm) bars. Cool before serving.

Makes 32 small bars.

Potato Cookies

Prince Edward Island is renowned for her potatoes, and clever cooks find many uses for them, including this cookie made with potato flour.

1/3 cup (75ml)	soft butter
1/3 cup (75ml)	brown sugar
1/3 cup (75ml)	sour cream
1/2 cup (125ml)	quick cooking oats
1/2 cup (125ml)	all-purpose flour
1/3 cup (75ml)	potato flour

Preheat oven to 375ºF (190ºC).

Cream together butter and sugar until light and fluffy. Beat in sour cream. In a separate bowl, combine oats and flours.

Stir flour mixture into creamed mixture in thirds. Form dough into 1-inch (2.5cm) balls and place on a parchment-lined cookie sheet.

Bake on the middle rack of the oven for 10 to 12 minutes or until edges are golden. Transfer to cooling racks.

Makes about 20 cookies.

Potato Flour Shortbread

Fine-textured potato flour gives this shortbread its soft feel.

1 cup (250ml)	soft butter
1/4 cup (50ml)	firmly packed brown sugar
1/4 cup (50ml)	granulated sugar
1 tbsp (15ml)	lemon juice
1 1/2 cups (375ml)	sifted all-purpose flour
1/2 cup (125ml)	potato flour

Preheat the oven to 300ºF (150ºC).

Cream together butter and sugars. Beat in lemon juice. Stir the flours together then stir into the wet ingredients until mixture is smooth.

Press dough into a straight-sided 9 1/2-inch (24cm) pie pan and prick with a fork.

Bake for 35 minutes or until edges are golden. Cut into 1 1/2-inch (4cm) wedges.

Makes 20 wedges.

Grammie Easter's Sugar Cookies

These cookies come from Joyce White of Hampshire, Prince Edward Island, and the recipe is reprinted with permission from The Guardian. Joyce writes, "These are cookies I have made over the years for all seasons. The children took lots of them to school, and my mom made them for us when we were in school."

1 cup (250ml)	shortening
1 cup (250ml)	brown sugar
1 cup (250ml)	granulated sugar
2	eggs
1 tsp (5ml)	vanilla
4 cups (1L)	flour
1/2 tsp (2ml)	salt
2 tbsp (25ml)	baking powder
1/2 cup (125ml)	sweet milk

Preheat oven to 325F (160ºC).

Cream together the shortening and sugars. Beat in eggs and vanilla. In a separate bowl, mix together flour, salt and baking powder. Add milk and dry ingredients to creamed shortening mixture, alternately in thirds .

Roll out dough on a lightly-floured surface to 1/8-inch (3mm) thickness. Cut into holiday shapes with 2-inch (5cm) cookie cutters and place on a greased cookie sheet, 1 inch (2.5cm) apart.

Bake for 10 minutes or until golden.

Transfer to a rack and cool for 5 minutes. Ice in holiday colours. If desired, make double cookies using jam or cooked raisins for a filling.

Makes 6 dozen cookies.

Rumballs

This recipe appeared on the Christmas Web site for the Prince Edward Island newspaper The Guardian, but there is no reason to hide these cookies away until Christmas. It was submitted by Edith Kandel of Crapaud, Prince Edward Island. We substituted graham cracker crumbs for the crushed cookie wafers that were called for in the original recipe.

2 cups (500ml)	graham cracker crumbs
1 cup (250ml)	chopped nuts
1 cup (250ml)	confectioners' sugar
2 tbsp (25ml)	cocoa
1/2 cup (125ml)	corn syrup
1/4 cup (50ml)	rum
1/4 cup (50ml)	chocolate sprinkles

In a medium bowl, combine cookie wafers, chopped nuts, sugar, and cocoa. Stir in syrup and rum. Shape dough into 1-inch (2.5cm) balls and roll in chocolate sprinkles to coat. Place in paper cups.

Makes about 3 dozen balls.

Stained-Glass Window Cookies

Gail Feehan of Cornwall, Prince Edward Island, submitted this recipe to The Guardian and they have graciously allowed me to reprint it here. The dough may be quite sticky — dust it liberally with flour while pressing it into shape.

1/2 lb (250g)	coloured hard candy
2/3 cup (150ml)	soft butter
1 cup (250ml)	granulated sugar
2	eggs
1/2 tsp (2ml)	vanilla
3 cups (750ml)	flour
2 tsp (10ml)	baking powder
1/2 tsp (2ml)	salt
1/3 cup (75ml)	milk

Preheat oven to 350ºF (180ºC).

Place candy in a plastic bag and crush with a mallet. Set aside.

Cream together butter and sugar. Beat in eggs and vanilla.

In a separate bowl, sift together flour, baking powder and salt. Add dry ingredients and milk to creamed butter, alternately in thirds.

Press out dough on a well-floured surface to 1/4-inch (5mm) thickness, and cut into 1x3-inch (2.5x8cm) strips. Arrange strips on a well-buttered baking sheet to form window frames. Distribute candy evenly inside frames.

Bake on middle rack of oven for 6 minutes or until the candy is melted. Let cool on cookie tray for 5 minutes or until the candy has hardened. Carefully lift cookies from the tray using a spatula.

Makes 8 very large cookies.

Molasses Cookies

Versions of this molasses cookie can be found in the regional cuisine of many provinces. Cooling the cookies on a rack allows the air to circulate around all surfaces, providing a quick, even dissipation of heat. This is important because as long as the cookie is hot, it will continue to cook.

1/2 cup (125ml)	soft butter
1/2 cup (125ml)	sugar
1/2 cup (125ml)	molasses
1 tsp (5ml)	vanilla
1 3/4 cups (425ml)	flour
1 tsp (5ml)	cinnamon
1/2 tsp (2ml)	ground ginger
1/2 tsp (2ml)	baking soda

In a medium, non-reactive pot, combine butter, sugar, molasses, and vanilla. Simmer over medium heat for 4 minutes. Set aside to cool.

Mix together flour, cinnamon, ginger, and baking soda. Stir cooled molasses mixture into flour mixture in thirds. Refrigerate for 30 minutes.

Preheat oven to 400ºF (200ºC).

Between two sheets of waxed paper, roll the dough out to 1/8-inch (3mm) thickness. Use 2-inch (5cm) cookie cutters to cut into desired shapes. Place 2 inches (5cm) apart on greased and floured cookie sheets.

Bake on the middle rack of the oven for 5 to 7 minutes or until edges are darkened. Transfer to cooling racks.

Makes about 3 dozen cookies.

Hermit Cookies

Hermit cookies were originally named for their extensive shelf life.
The strong spices were thought to taste better after a few days.

1/2 cup (125ml)	soft butter
1 cup (250ml)	firmly packed golden sugar
1	egg
2 tbsp (25ml)	whipping cream
1 tsp (5ml)	vanilla
1 1/2 cups (375ml)	all-purpose flour
1 tsp (5ml)	baking powder
1 tsp (5ml)	ground cloves
1 tsp (5ml)	cinnamon
1/2 tsp (2ml)	freshly-grated nutmeg
1/4 tsp (1ml)	salt
1 cup (250ml)	raisins
1/4 cup (50ml)	candied lemon

Preheat oven to 375ºF (190ºC).

Cream together butter and sugar until light and fluffy. Beat in egg, cream, and vanilla. In a separate bowl, combine flour, baking powder, cloves, cinnamon, nutmeg, and salt.

Stir flour mixture into creamed mixture in thirds. Fold in raisins and candied lemon. Drop heaping tablespoons of dough 3 inches (8cm) apart on a greased cookie sheet.

Bake on the middle rack of the oven for 10 to 12 minutes or until edges are darkened. Transfer to cooling racks.

Makes about 2 dozen cookies.

The Great Canadian Cookie Contest

We all know that homemade cookies are the best of the best. Time-tested recipes, perfected over generations, are kept in family archives because they meet the tough standards of your critics — kids and kids at heart. For this reason my book could never be complete without you, the home bakers — and the best bakers.

Canadian Online Explorer (CANOE) is Canada's leading Internet network with more than 3.6 million users and more than 60 million page views each month. Lifewise, the CANOE area devoted to — but not exclusively for — Canadian women was launched in January 2000. Lifewise covers fashion, beauty, diet, fitness, home decor, food, and wine, with thousands of recipes, reviews, and entertaining ideas. As a contributor to Lifewise, I suggested we ask readers to e-mail their favourite cookie recipes to us. We called it the Great Canadian Cookie Contest, and the response was terrific. The cookies were rated on taste, texture, appearance, aroma, originality, and quality of ingredients. I tested all the entries and came up with three runners up and one winner. Choosing just one winner was the most difficult part, because there were so many fantastic cookies. I've selected the best of the entries for this chapter.

And the winner is ...

Oatmeal Raisin Chocolate Chip Cookies

Jeanne Fulop writes:
"I hope you love these cookies as much as my family does."

2 1/3 cups (575ml)	quick-cooking oats
1 1/2 cups (375ml)	all-purpose flour
2 tsp (10ml)	baking soda
1 tsp (5ml)	salt
1 cup (250ml)	soft butter
1 1/2 cups (375ml)	packed brown sugar
2	eggs
1 tsp (5ml)	vanilla
1 1/2 cups (375ml)	semi-sweet chocolate chips
1 cup (250ml)	raisins

In a large bowl, combine oats, flour, baking soda, and salt.

In a separate bowl, cream together butter and sugar until light and fluffy. Beat in eggs, one at a time, then add vanilla.

Stir flour mixture into creamed mixture in thirds. Fold in chocolate chips and raisins. Refrigerate dough for 1 hour.

Preheat oven to 350°F (180°C).

Drop tablespoons of dough 2 inches (5cm) apart on a greased cookie sheet.

Bake on the middle rack of the oven for 12 to 15 minutes or until golden. Cool for 5 minutes on cookie sheet, then transfer to cooling racks. Store in an airtight container or freeze for up to 1 month. Enjoy with a smile.

Makes about 4 dozen cookies.

Chocolate Coffee Cookies

Tony Lopez submitted the recipe for this delicious cookie It has a fantastic full flavour and the combination of chocolate and coffee is almost irresistible.

1 cup (250ml)	soft butter
1 cup (250ml)	granulated sugar
1 cup (250ml)	brown sugar
2	eggs
1/4 cup (50ml)	half-and-half (10%) cream
2 tsp (10ml)	instant coffee
2 tsp (10ml)	Kahlúa™
2 cups (500ml)	all-purpose flour
1 tsp (5ml)	baking powder
1/2 tsp (2ml)	baking soda
1/2 tsp (2ml)	salt
2 1/4 cups (550ml)	quick-cooking oats
1/2 cup (125ml)	semi-sweet dark chocolate chips

Cream together butter and sugars until light and fluffy. Beat in eggs, one at a time, then cream, coffee and Kahlúa.

Sift together flour, baking powder, baking soda, and salt. Stir in oats and chocolate chips. Fold dry ingredients into creamed mixture in thirds. Refrigerate for 1 hour.

Preheat oven to 350ºF (180ºC).

Roll dough into 1-inch (2.5cm) balls and set 1 inch (2.5cm) apart on a parchment-lined cookie sheet.

Bake for 7 to 10 minutes or until edges are darkened. Cool on cookie sheet for 2 minutes, then transfer to cooling racks.

Makes about 8 dozen cookies.

Island Shortbread Jewels

This recipe for this pretty cookie was sent to us by Chico Dedick of Delta, British Columbia. Chico writes, "This recipe was given to me during our stay in the British West Indies. The cookies are delicious!"

1 cup (250ml)	soft butter
1/4 cup (50ml)	granulated sugar
1 tsp (5ml)	vanilla
2 cups (500ml)	sifted all-purpose flour
1/4 tsp (1ml)	salt
2 cups (500ml)	flaked, unsweetened coconut
3/4 cup (175ml)	powdered sugar
3/4 cup (175ml)	fruit jelly
	(guava, raspberry or black currant)

Preheat oven to 300ºF (160ºC).

Using a mixer, cream together butter and sugar until light and fluffy. Beat in vanilla. In a separate bowl, combine flour and salt. Stir dry ingredients into creamed mixture in thirds. Fold in coconut.

Shape dough into walnut-sized balls and place 2 inches (5cm) apart on a greased baking sheet. Using a fingertip or the handle of a wooden spoon, make a small depression in the centre of each cookie.

Bake on the middle rack of the oven for 20 to 25 minutes or until the cookies begin to darken.

Sift powdered sugar onto a sheet of waxed paper. Transfer the hot cookies to the waxed paper, dust with additional sugar, and place a dollop of jelly in the centre of each cookie. Transfer to cooling racks.

Makes about 3 dozen cookies .

Bird's Nest Cookies

This is Celina Hsueh's favourite family recipe. This cookie doesn't just look pretty;
it melts in your mouth. (My cookies must have been larger than Celina's because I only
got 2 dozen.) You may want to substitute butter for the vegetable shortening.

1 cup (250ml)	vegetable shortening
1/2 cup (125ml)	sugar
1	large egg, separated
1	large egg yolk
1 1/2 tsp (7ml)	vanilla essence
2 cups (500ml)	all-purpose flour
1/4 tsp (1ml)	salt
1 cup (250ml)	finely chopped walnuts OR pecans
36	chocolate kisses

Preheat oven to 375°F (190°C).

Combine the flour and salt. In a large mixing bowl, cream together shortening and sugar until light and fluffy. Beat in the egg yolks and the vanilla. Stir the flour mixture into the creamed mixture in thirds.

In a shallow bowl, beat the egg white until frothy. Spread the chopped nuts on a piece of waxed or grease-proof paper. Roll dough into 1-inch (2.5cm) balls. Dip each ball in egg white to coat, then roll in chopped nuts. Place 1 inch (2.5cm) apart on ungreased cookie sheets. Using a finger, make a small depression in the centre of each ball.

Bake on the middle rack of the oven, for 12 to 15 minutes or until lightly coloured. Press an upside down chocolate kiss into the centre of each hot cookie, then transfer to wire racks.

Makes 3 dozen cookies.

Boston Date Drops

Mary Beesley of Oakville, Ontario, informs us that this old, family recipe comes from her mother's recipe box. The dates and spices — particularly the strong taste of cloves — give this rich cookie its unique taste. You may want to substitute butter for the margarine.

1 tsp (5ml)	baking soda
2/3 cup (150ml)	margarine
1 cup (250ml)	firmly packed brown sugar
2	eggs
1 1/2–1 2/3 (375–400ml)	cups pastry flour
1 tsp (5ml)	ground cloves
1/2 tsp (2ml)	cinnamon
1/2 tsp (2ml)	freshly grated nutmeg
1 lb (500g)	chopped dates
1/2 lb (250g)	chopped nuts
1 cup (250ml)	(2 handfuls) corn flakes

Preheat oven to 350ºF (180ºC).

Dissolve baking soda in 1 tbsp (15ml) hot water. Cream together margarine and sugar until light and fluffy. Beat in eggs, then stir in baking soda.

In a separate bowl, combine flour, cloves, cinnamon, and nutmeg. Stir flour mixture into creamed mixture in thirds. Fold in dates and nuts, then corn flakes.

Drop rounded tablespoons of dough on a greased cookie sheet.

Bake on the middle rack of the oven for 10 minutes or until golden.

Makes about 2 dozen cookies.

Cathy's Chocolate Chip Cookies

Coconut is an interesting addition to this chewy cookie submitted by Cathy Friedel of Fairview, Alberta.

1 cup (250ml)	soft butter
1/2 cup (125ml)	granulated sugar
1 cup (250ml)	brown sugar
1	egg
1 tsp (5ml)	vanilla
1 1/2 cups (375ml)	flour
1 tsp (5ml)	baking powder
1 tsp (5ml)	baking soda
1 1/2 cups (375ml)	oatmeal
1 cup (250ml)	sweetened coconut
1 cup (250ml)	semi-sweet chocolate chips

Preheat oven to 350°F (180°C).

Cream together butter and sugars until light and fluffy. Beat in egg, then vanilla.

In a separate bowl, combine flour with baking powder and baking soda. Stir flour mixture into creamed mixture in thirds. Fold in oatmeal, coconut, and chocolate chips.

Roll into 1-inch (2.5cm) balls and place 2 inches (5cm) apart on a parchment-lined cookie sheet.

Bake for 10 to 12 minutes or until light brown. Cool on cookie sheet for 2 minutes, then transfer to cooling racks.

Makes 40 cookies.

Orange Cookies

This deceptively plain little cookie has a pleasant orange flavour, and it scored high on taste. Mal Cohen of Dartmouth, Nova Scotia, admitted to stealing the recipe from his wife Marlies. You may want to substitute butter for the margarine.

1 cup (250ml)	margarine
1 cup (250ml)	sugar
1	egg
1 tbsp (15ml)	grated orange zest
1 tsp (5ml)	orange juice
2 1/2 cups (625ml)	all-purpose flour
1/2 tsp (2ml)	baking powder

Cream together margarine and sugar until light and fluffy. Beat in egg, then orange zest and juice.

In a separate bowl, combine flour and baking powder. Stir flour mixture into creamed mixture in thirds. Roll dough into a 1 1/2- to 2-inch (4 to 5cm) log and refrigerate for 1 hour.

Preheat oven to 375ºF (190ºC).

Cut log into 1/2-inch (1cm) slices and place 1 1/2 inches (4cm) apart on an ungreased cookie sheet.

Bake on the middle rack of the oven for 9 minutes or until edges are golden. Cool on cookie sheet for 2 minutes, then transfer to cooling racks.

Makes about 4 dozen cookies.

Carrot Cookies

Sylvie Schryburt of Ottawa, Ontario, translated the original French version of her recipe into English for us. I think the best thing about this cookie is that it is a really creative way to entice the tot set to eat carrots!

1 cup (250ml)	soft butter
3/4 cup (175ml)	sugar
1	egg, beaten
1 tsp (5ml)	vanilla
2 cups (500ml)	flour
1 tsp (5ml)	baking powder
1 cup (250ml)	cooked carrots, mashed and cooled

GLAZE

1 cup (250ml)	icing sugar
1 tbsp (15ml)	soft butter
1 tbsp (15ml)	finely grated orange zest
Juice of 1	orange

Preheat oven to 375°F (190°C).

Cream together butter and sugar until light and fluffy. Beat in egg, then vanilla. In a separate bowl, sift together flour and baking powder.

Stir flour mixture and carrots into creamed mixture, alternately in thirds. Drop tablespoons of dough 2 inches (5cm) apart onto a greased cookie sheet.

Bake on the middle rack of the oven for 8 to 10 minutes or until firm. Cool for 2 minutes on cookie sheets, then transfer to cooling racks.

Whisk together icing sugar, butter, and orange zest and juice until smooth. Spread over cooled cookies.

Makes about 3 dozen cookies.

Family Cookies

Gwen Baskin of Edmonton, Alberta wrote, "This is a valued family recipe, that has been passed down from daughter to daughter. Hope you enjoy." You may want to substitute butter for the margarine.

1 cup (250ml)	margarine
1 cup (250ml)	brown sugar
3/4 cup (175ml)	granulated sugar
2	eggs
1 tsp (5ml)	vanilla
2 cups (500ml)	flour
1 tsp (5ml)	baking soda
1/2 tsp (2ml)	baking powder
1/8 tsp (.5ml)	salt
2 cups (500ml)	corn flakes
1 cup (250ml)	oats

Preheat oven to 350°F (180°C).

Cream together margarine and sugars until light and fluffy. Beat in eggs, then vanilla. In a separate bowl, combine flour, baking soda, baking powder and salt.

Stir flour mixture into creamed mixture in thirds. Fold in corn flakes and oats. Drop rounded tablespoons of dough 2 inches (5cm) apart on a greased cookie sheet.

Bake on the middle rack of the oven for 4 minutes, turn, and bake for an additional 4 minutes or until edges are golden. Cool on cookie sheet for 2 minutes, then transfer to cooling racks.

Makes about 3 dozen cookies.

The Great Health Cookie

This recipe was sent in by best friends, Karin Deschamps and Marilyn Leis of Torrington, Alberta. Karin insists that "Marilyn is the best baker around these parts!" Well, here's to great friendships and great cookies. You may want to substitute butter for the margarine.

1 cup (250ml)	whole wheat flour
1/4 cup (50ml)	toasted wheat germ
1/4 cup (50ml)	bran
1 tsp (5ml)	baking powder
1/2 tsp (2ml)	salt
1/4 tsp (1ml)	cinnamon
1/4 tsp (1ml)	freshly grated nutmeg
1/8 tsp (.5ml)	ground cloves
1 cup (250ml)	margarine
1 cup (250ml)	brown sugar
2	eggs
2 cups (500ml)	rolled oats
1/2 cup (125ml)	walnuts
1/2 cup (125ml)	sunflower seeds
1/2 cup (125ml)	raisins

Preheat oven to 350ºF (180ºC).

Stir together flour, wheat germ, bran, baking powder, salt, cinnamon, nutmeg, and cloves and set aside. Cream together margarine and sugar until light and fluffy. Beat in eggs, one at a time.

Stir flour mixture into creamed mixture in thirds. Fold in oats, walnuts, sunflower seeds, and raisins. Roll into 1-inch (2.5cm) balls and place 2 inches (5cm) apart on a greased cookie sheet.

Bake for 8 to 12 minutes or until edges are golden. Cool on cookie sheet for 2 minutes, then transfer to cooling racks.

Makes about 3 dozen cookies.

Peanut Blossoms

Shannon Vinter of Regina, Saskatchewan, has taken a classic peanut butter cookie and dressed it up with a chocolate rosebud. You may want to substitute butter for the margarine.

1/2 cup (125ml)	margarine
1/2 cup (125ml)	granulated sugar
1/2 cup (125ml)	brown sugar
1/2 cup (125ml)	peanut butter
1	egg
2 tbsp (25ml)	milk
1 tsp (5ml)	vanilla
1 3/4 cups (425ml)	flour
1 tsp (5ml)	baking soda
1/4 tsp (1ml)	salt
1/4 cup (50ml)	white decorators' sugar
36	chocolate rosebuds

Preheat oven to 350ºF (180ºC).

Cream together margarine and sugars until light and fluffy. Beat in peanut butter, then egg, milk, and vanilla.

In a separate bowl, sift together flour, baking soda, and salt. Stir flour mixture into peanut mixture in thirds.

Form dough into scant 1-inch (2.5cm) balls. Roll each ball in decorators' sugar, then place 1 1/2 inches (4cm) apart on an ungreased cookie sheet.

Bake on middle rack of oven for 8 to 10 minutes or until golden. Remove from oven and place one chocolate rosebud in the centre of each cookie while still warm. Transfer to cooling racks.

Makes about 3 dozen cookies.

Chewy Chocolate Chippers

Kevin Robertson of Greenwood, Nova Scotia sent in this recipe for a standard oatmeal chocolate chip cookie. But then, you can never have enough chocolate chip cookies. You may want to substitute butter for the margarine.

1/2 cup (125ml)	margarine, softened
1 cup (250ml)	lightly packed brown sugar
1	egg
1/2 tsp (2ml)	vanilla
1 cup (250ml)	flour
1 cup (250ml)	rolled oats
1/2 tsp (2ml)	baking soda
1/4 tsp (1ml)	salt
1 cup (250ml)	chocolate chips

Preheat oven to 350ºF (180ºC).

Cream together margarine and sugar until light and fluffy. Beat in egg and vanilla.

In a separate bowl, combine flour with oats, baking soda and salt. Stir flour mixture into creamed mixture in thirds. Fold in chocolate chips.

Drop rounded tablespoons of dough onto a greased cookie sheet.

Bake on the middle rack of the oven for 8 to 10 minutes or until edges are golden. Cool on cookie sheet for 2 minutes, then transfer to cooling racks.

Makes about 2 dozen cookies.

Crunchy Crispy Cookies

*Phyllis Marchment of Victoria, British Columbia, sent in this recipe
for her favourite drop cookie. The combination of granola, brown sugar,
and coconut creates a pleasantly hearty cookie.*

1 cup (250ml)	soft butter
1 cup (250ml)	brown sugar
1	egg
1 tsp (5ml)	vanilla
1 1/2 cups (375ml)	all-purpose flour
2 tsp (10ml)	baking powder
1/4 tsp (1ml)	baking soda
1/4 tsp (1ml)	salt
1 cup (250ml)	unsweetened coconut
3/4 cup (175ml)	quick-cooking oats
1/2 cup (125ml)	granola

Preheat oven to 350ºF (180ºC).

Cream together butter and sugar. Beat in egg and vanilla.

In a separate bowl, combine flour with baking powder, baking soda, and salt. Stir in coconut, oats, and granola. Stir flour mixture into creamed mixture in thirds.

Drop rounded tablespoons of dough 2 inches (5cm) apart on a greased baking sheet, and lightly flatten with a fork dipped in cold water.

Bake on the middle rack of the oven for 9 to 12 minutes or until golden. Cool on cookie sheet for 2 minutes, then transfer to cooling racks.

Makes about 30 cookies.

Chewy Peanut Butter Chocolate Chip Cookes

Sue Belliveau of Kanata, Ontario, came right out and told me that these are the best cookies anyone has ever tasted. Well, it's one big cookie and it certainly gained support with my kid testers.

1/2 cup (125ml)	soft butter
1/2 cup (125ml)	peanut butter
1 cup (250ml)	brown sugar
1/2 cup (125ml)	granulated sugar
2	eggs
2 tbsp (25ml)	corn syrup
2 tbsp (25ml)	water
2 tsp (10ml)	vanilla
2 1/2 cups (625ml)	all-purpose flour
1 tsp (5ml)	baking soda
1/2 tsp (2ml)	salt
2 cups (500ml)	semi-sweet chocolate chips

Preheat oven to 375ºF (190ºC).

In a large bowl, cream together butter, peanut butter, and sugars. Beat in eggs, one at time, followed by corn syrup, water, and vanilla.

In a separate bowl, combine flour, baking soda and salt. Stir flour mixture into creamed mixture in thirds. Fold in chocolate chips. Drop 2 rounded tablespoons of dough 3 inches (8cm) apart on a parchment-lined cookie sheet.

Bake on the middle rack of the oven for 12 to 14 minutes or until golden. Cool on cookie sheet for 2 minutes, then transfer to cooling racks.

Makes about 2 dozen large cookies.

One Smart Cookie

Another chocolate chip cookie! And a good one with the added texture and flavour of butterscotch and pecans. This recipe comes from Pat Pfimmer of Huntsville, Ontario, who says, "We have enjoyed variations of this recipe for twenty years. Enjoy!" Grind the oatmeal in a food processor until it resembles coarse crumbs.

1 lb (500g)	shortening
1 cup (250ml)	granulated sugar
1 cup (250ml)	brown sugar
2	eggs
1 tsp (5ml)	vanilla
3 cups (750ml)	all-purpose flour
2 tsp (10ml)	baking soda
3 1/4 cups (800ml)	ground quick-cooking oatmeal
1 cup (250ml)	chocolate chips
1 cup (250ml)	butterscotch chips
3/4 cup (175ml)	chopped pecans

Preheat oven to 350ºF (180ºC).

Cream together shortening and sugars. Bean in eggs, one at a time, then vanilla.

In a separate bowl, combine flour, baking soda, and ground oatmeal. Stir the flour mixture into the creamed mixture in thirds. Fold in chocolate chips, butterscotch chips, and pecans.

Roll tablespoon-sized pieces into balls and place 3 inches (8cm) apart on a parchment-lined cookie sheet. Flatten cookies with the bottom of a glass dipped in cold water.

Bake on the middle rack of the oven for 10 to 12 minutes or until golden. Cool on cookie sheet for 2 minutes, then transfer to cooling racks.

Makes about 5 dozen cookies.

Walnut Chocolate Chip Cookies

Janet McCammon of Winnipeg, Manitoba, sent in her recipe for these winning cookies.
The addition of walnuts gives the chocolate chip theme — everyone's favourite —
a nice grown up edge. In fact Janet suggests eliminating the walnuts if baking for anyone
under the age of fifteen. Janet also suggests spreading the cookies on brown
paper bags to cool, as an alternative to cooling racks.

1 1/2 cups (375ml)	flour
3/4 tsp (4ml)	baking soda
1/2 tsp (2ml)	salt
3/4 cup (175ml)	soft butter
1/2 cup (125ml)	granulated sugar
1/2 cup (125ml)	brown sugar
1	egg
1/2 tsp (2ml)	vanilla
1 cup (250ml)	semi-sweet chocolate chips
1 cup (250ml)	chopped walnuts

Preheat oven to 375ºF (190ºC).

Combine flour, baking soda, and salt.

In a large bowl, cream together butter and sugars until light and fluffy. Beat in egg, then vanilla. Stir flour mixture into creamed mixture in thirds. Fold in chocolate chips and walnuts.

Drop teaspoons of dough 2 inches (5cm) apart on a greased cookie sheet.

Bake on the middle rack of the oven for 8 to 10 minutes or until golden. Cool on cookie sheet for 2 minutes, then transfer to cooling racks.

Makes 5 dozen small cookies.

Sour Cream Cookies

This recipe was sent in by Lash MacLeod of Sherwood Park, Alberta. I am a big fan of cakey cookies, so this cinnamon-dusted treat suited me nicely.

3 cups (750ml)	all-purpose flour
1 tsp (5ml)	salt
1 tsp (5ml)	baking powder
1/2 tsp (2ml)	baking soda
1/2 cup (125ml)	soft butter
1 1/2 cups (375ml)	sugar
2	eggs
1 tsp (5ml)	vanilla
1 cup (250ml)	sour cream
1 tbsp (15ml)	sugar (for dusting)
1 tsp (5ml)	cinnamon (for dusting)

Preheat oven to 400ºF (200ºC).

Combine flour, salt, baking powder, and baking soda.

In a large bowl, cream together butter and sugar until light and fluffy. Beat in eggs, one at a time, then vanilla. Stir flour mixture and sour cream into creamed mixture, alternately in thirds.

Drop rounded tablespoons of dough 3 inches (8cm) apart onto a parchment-lined cookie sheet. Combine remaining sugar and cinnamon and dust the top of the cookies .

Bake on the middle rack of the oven for 5 to 8 minutes or until edges are golden. Cool on cookie sheet for 2 minutes, then transfer to cooling racks.

Makes about 5 dozen cookies.

Mom's Chocolate Chip Cookies

Elaine Eagles of Riverview, New Brunswick, writes, "This is the cookie recipe that my mother used to make for us when we were growing up. I think it's great, so try it out!" Well, Elaine, I enjoyed your mom's recipe for these nice, thin cookies. The high quantity of brown sugar gives them a rich flavour, almost like molasses.

3/4 cup (175ml)	shortening
2 cups (500ml)	brown sugar
2	eggs
1 tsp (5ml)	vanilla
1 tsp (5ml)	baking soda
2 1/2 cups (625ml)	all-purpose flour
1 tsp (5ml)	salt
8 oz (250g)	milk chocolate chips

Preheat oven to 350ºF (180ºC).

Dissolve baking soda in 1/4 cup (50ml) of boiling water. Cream together shortening and sugar until light and fluffy. Beat in eggs, one at a time, then vanilla and dissolved baking soda.

In a separate bowl, combine flour and salt. Stir flour mixture into creamed mixture in thirds. Fold in chocolate chips. Drop rounded tablespoons 3 inches (8cm) apart on a parchment-lined cookie sheet.

Bake on the middle rack of the oven for 10 to 15 minutes or until golden.

Makes about 4 1/2 dozen cookies.

Old-Fashioned Chocolate Chip Cookies

Shelley DeLong of Fort McMurray, Alberta, says, "This is the best chocolate chip cookie I have ever had or made." It lives up to its name and could easily be the prototype to the original Toll House cookie.

1 cup (250ml)	shortening
1 cup (250ml)	brown sugar
1/2 cup (125ml)	granulated sugar
1 tsp (5ml)	vanilla
2 cups (500ml)	flour
1 tsp (5ml)	baking soda
1 tsp (5ml)	salt
1 cup (250ml)	chocolate chips

Preheat oven to 375ºF (190ºC).

Cream together shortening and sugars until light and fluffy. Beat in vanilla.

In a separate bowl, combine flour, baking soda and salt. Stir flour mixture into creamed mixture in thirds. Fold in chocolate chips.

Drop even tablespoons of dough 3 inches (8cm) apart on a greased cookie sheet.

Bake on the middle rack of the oven for 8 to 10 minutes or until golden. Cool on cookie sheet for 2 minutes, then transfer to cooling racks.

Makes about 4 dozen cookies.

Peanut Butter Cookies

Ann Richardson of St. Thomas, Ontario, writes, "This recipe was given to me by my husband's grandma. I made it for my kids, and now I make it for my grandkids." Well, a recipe with that kind of legacy can hardly be passed up.

1/2 cup (125ml)	soft butter
1/2 cup (125ml)	peanut butter
1/2 cup (125ml)	granulated sugar
1/2 cup (125ml)	brown sugar
1	egg
1/2 tsp (2ml)	vanilla
1 cup (250ml)	all-purpose flour
1/2 tsp (2ml)	baking soda

Preheat oven to 350ºF (180ºC).

Cream together butter, peanut butter, and sugars until light and fluffy. Beat in egg, then vanilla.

In a separate bowl, combine flour and baking soda. Stir flour mixture into creamed mixture, in thirds.

Drop teaspoons of dough 2 inches (5cm) apart on a parchment-lined cookie sheet. Make a criss-cross pattern on each cookie with a floured fork.

Bake on the middle rack of the oven for 10 to 12 minutes or until edges are golden. Cool on cookie sheet for 2 minutes, then transfer to cooling racks.

Makes about 30 cookies.

Sweet-and-Easy Sugar Cookies

Brenda Detta of Powassan, Ontario, says "I got this recipe from my mom's old recipe book. I make these cookies for friends at Christmas and they always ask for more." You may want to substitute butter for the margarine.

2 cups (500ml)	margarine
2 cups (500ml)	sugar
2	eggs
4 cups (1L)	all-purpose flour
4 tsp (20ml)	cream of tartar
2 tsp (10ml)	baking soda
2 cups (500ml)	chocolate chips

Preheat oven to 350°F (180°C).

Cream margarine and sugar until light and fluffy. Beat in eggs.

In a separate bowl, combine flour, cream of tartar, and baking soda. Stir flour mixture into creamed mixture in thirds. Fold in chocolate chips.

Shape dough into 1-inch (2.5cm) balls and place 2 inches (5cm) apart on a greased cookie sheet.

Bake on the middle rack of the oven for 12 to 15 minutes or until edges are lightly browned. Cool on cookie sheet for 2 minutes, then transfer to cooling racks.

Makes about 5 dozen small cookies.

Faith's Peanut Butter Cookies

Jack Stiff of Scarborough, Ontario, writes "Twenty-two years ago, my wife, Faith was recovering in hospital after a near-fatal illness. As part of her occupational therapy, she had to type out and bake a recipe. The cookie's wonderful aroma attracted doctors, nurses and other hospital staff. She brought the recipe home with her and we still follow that dog-eared original record card. Warning—this recipe is addictive. Better make two batches at once."

1/2 cup (125ml)	shortening
1/2 cup (125ml)	peanut butter
1/2 cup (125ml)	lightly packed brown sugar
1	egg
1/2 tsp (2ml)	vanilla
1 1/4 cups (300ml)	flour
1 tsp (5ml)	baking soda
1/2 tsp (2ml)	salt

Preheat oven to 350ºF (180ºC).

Cream together shortening, peanut butter and sugar until light and fluffy. Beat in egg, then vanilla.

In a separate bowl, combine flour, baking soda and salt. Stir flour mixture into creamed mixture in thirds.

Shape dough into 1-inch (2.5cm) balls and place 2 inches (5cm) apart on an ungreased cookie sheet. Flatten slightly with a fork dipped in cold water.

Bake on the middle rack of the oven for 10 to 15 minutes or until edges are golden. Cool on cookie sheet for 2 minutes, then transfer to cooling racks.

Makes about 2 dozen cookies.

Rolly Ball Cookies

Karen MacDonald of Amherst, Nova Scotia, writes, "This recipe is a favourite at our house. The name Rolly Ball Cookies came from my youngest." What impressed me about this recipe is its absolute simplicity — I've never seen one like it. These cookies are very sweet but that probably adds to their appeal for little ones. It's a great recipe to have for friends and family who are allergic to wheat.

1 cup (250ml)	sugar
1 cup (250ml)	peanut butter
1	egg

Preheat oven to 325°F (170°C).

Beat sugar, peanut butter, and egg together. Roll into 1-inch (2.5cm) balls and place 2 inches (5cm) apart on a parchment-lined cookie sheet. Flatten each ball slightly with a fork dipped in cold water.

Bake on the middle rack of the oven for 8 minutes.

Makes about 30 small cookies.

Anna's Amazing Chocolate Chunk Cookies

Anna Szczepaniak of Toronto, writes, "I invented this recipe one day and it continues to be a hit with my friends." It seems that the great Canadian tradition of cookie invention is alive and well.

3/4 cup (175ml)	soft butter
1 cup (250ml)	firmly packed brown sugar
1	egg
1 tsp (5ml)	vanilla
2 cups (500ml)	unbleached all-purpose flour
1 tsp (5ml)	cinnamon
1 tsp (5ml)	baking soda
1/2 tsp (2ml)	salt
1 cup (250ml)	rolled oats
1 cup (250ml)	unsweetened, shredded coconut
1 cup (250ml)	butterscotch chips
1 cup (250ml)	chopped pecans
7 oz (200g)	semi-sweet chocolate squares, cut into chunks

Preheat oven to 350°F (180°C).

Cream together butter and sugar until light and fluffy. Beat in egg, then vanilla.

In a separate bowl, sift together flour, cinnamon, baking soda and salt. Stir in oats and coconut. Stir flour mixture into creamed mixture in thirds. Fold in chips, pecans, and chocolate.

Drop tablespoons of dough 3 inches (8cm) apart on an ungreased cookie sheet.

Bake on the middle rack of the oven for 9 to 12 minutes or until bottoms are lightly browned. Cool on cookie sheet for 2 minutes, then transfer to cooling racks.

Makes about 24 large cookies.

Angela's Hazelnut Cookies

Angela Klyne of Vaughan, Ontario, sent us her recipe for these elegant treats.
She has done a terrific job of building flavours here — hazelnut layered with citrus
zest and spices — and the use of cake flour makes this a delicate cookie.

3	eggs
1 cup (250ml)	sugar
2/3 cups (150ml)	oil
Juice and zest of 1	orange
Juice and zest of 1	lemon
2 1/2 cups (625ml)	cake flour
1/2 cup (125ml)	finely chopped hazelnuts
1 tbsp (15ml)	baking powder
1/4 tsp (1ml)	nutmeg
1 tsp (5ml)	cinnamon (for dusting)
1 tbsp (15ml)	sugar (for dusting)

Preheat oven to 350°F (180°C).

In a food processor, process eggs, sugar, oil, juices, and zest for 30 seconds. Add flour, hazelnuts, baking powder, and nutmeg and process until combined.

Turn out the dough on a well-floured surface and shape into logs 1 inch (2.5cm) thick and 4 inches (10cm) long. Place logs 2 inches (5cm) apart on a greased cookie sheet. Combine cinnamon and sugar and dust logs.

Bake on the middle rack of the oven for 30 to 40 minutes or until golden.

Remove from the oven. Using a wet knife, cut logs into 1/2-inch (1cm) slices. Place slices on cookie sheet

Bake for 5 to 10 minutes or until the slices are crisp. Cool on cookie sheet for 2 minutes, then transfer to cooling racks.

Makes about 3 dozen cookies.

Scandinavian Cookies

Denise Taylor of Campbell River, British Columbia, writes, "These are so good, I always double the recipe, and they are a tradition at Christmas."

1/2 cup (125ml)	soft butter
1/4 cup (50ml)	brown sugar
1 cup (250ml)	sifted all-purpose flour
1	egg white
1/2 cup (125ml)	finely chopped nuts
1/2 cup (125ml)	chocolate icing

Preheat oven to 350°F (180°C).

Cream together butter and sugar until light and fluffy. Stir in flour. Form dough into walnut-sized balls.

Beat egg white to a light foam. Dip balls in egg white, then roll in nuts to coat. Place balls 2 inches (5cm) apart on a greased cookie sheet. Press a small hollow in each one.

Bake on the middle rack of the oven for 15 to 18 minutes or until edges are golden. Cool on cookie sheet for 2 minutes, then transfer to cooling racks. Once cool, place a dab of chocolate icing in the hollow of each cookie.

Makes about 2 dozen small cookies.

Apricot Cookies

This recipe comes from Lois Ireland of Port Elgin, Ontario. Apricots, almond, and coconut — the dominant flavours — give this cookie a tropical twist.

1 cup (250ml)	dried chopped apricots
1/2 cup (125ml)	water
1 cup (250ml)	shortening
1/2 cup (125ml)	brown sugar
1/2 cup (125ml)	granulated sugar
1	egg
1 tsp (5ml)	vanilla
1/4 tsp (1ml)	almond extract
1 3/4 cups (425ml)	all-purpose flour
2 tsp (10ml)	baking powder
1/2 tsp (2ml)	salt
1 1/2 cups (375ml)	shredded coconut

In a small saucepan over medium heat, cook apricots in water for 10 minutes or until soft. Set aside to cool.

Preheat oven to 375°F (190°C).

Cream together shortening and sugars until light and fluffy. Beat in egg, then vanilla and almond extract. In a separate bowl, sift together flour, baking powder, and salt.

Stir flour mixture into creamed mixture in thirds. Fold in apricots. Form dough into 1-inch (2.5cm) balls and roll in coconut to coat. Place balls 2 inches (5cm) apart on a greased cookie sheet.

Bake on the middle rack of the oven for 15 to 20 minutes or until coconut is toasted.

Makes about 4 dozen small cookies.

Shortbread Cookies

Kathy Blommaert of Dresden, Ontario, writes, "This is a recipe my grandma got from Scotland years ago. She's now in a nursing home but I still make these cookies for her. They're our family favourite at Christmas time." These simple, basic cookies can be prettied up by dusting with raw sugar or coloured decorators' sugar before baking.

1 lb (500g)	soft butter
1 cup (250ml)	sugar
1/2 cup (125ml)	rice flour
3–4 cups (750ml–1L)	pastry flour

Preheat oven to 350ºF (180ºC).

Cream together butter and sugar until light and fluffy. Stir in rice flour. Stir in flour until the dough is firm enough to roll easily.

Roll out on a floured surface to 1/4 inch (5mm) thick. Cut with cookie cutters as desired and place cookies 1 1/2 inches (4cm) apart on a parchment-lined cookie sheet.

Bake on the middle rack of the oven for 15 to 18 minutes or until golden.

Makes 4 to 5 dozen cookies (depending on the size of the cutters).

Banana Cookies

This recipe was submitted by Kim Hayward of Elliot Lake, Ontario.
Bananas add moisture, tenderness and flavour to this chocolate chip cookie.
You may want to substitute butter for the margarine.

2 1/4 cups (550ml)	all-purpose flour
2 tsp (10ml)	baking powder
1/2 tsp (2ml)	salt
1/4 tsp (1ml)	baking soda
2/3 cup (150ml)	margarine
1 cup (250ml)	sugar
2	eggs
1 tsp (5ml)	vanilla
1 cup (250ml)	mashed, ripe bananas
1 cup (250ml)	chocolate chips

Preheat oven to 400ºF (200ºC).

Combine flour, baking powder, salt and baking soda.

In a large bowl, cream together margarine and sugar until light and fluffy. Beat in eggs, one at a time, then vanilla and banana. Stir flour mixture into creamed mixture in thirds. Fold in chocolate chips.

Drop teaspoons of dough 2 inches (5cm) apart on a greased cookie sheet.

Bake on the middle rack of the oven for 10 to 15 minutes or until golden. Cool on cookie sheet for 2 minutes, then transfer to cooling racks.

Makes 5 dozen small cookies.

Chocolate Haystacks-on-the-Run

Jennifer Rayment of Richmond Hill, Ontario, sent in her recipe for these fun-loving cookies. No-bake cookies like these are great to make with small children helping.

3/4 cup (175ml)	semi-sweet chocolate chips
2 tbsp (25ml)	milk
2 tbsp (25ml)	corn syrup or soft butter
1 1/2 cups (375ml)	corn flakes
3/4 cup (175ml)	sweetened, flaked coconut

In a double boiler or stainless steel bowl over hot (not boiling) water, melt chocolate chips with milk and corn syrup. Remove from heat.

In a separate bowl, coarsely crush corn flakes. Add coconut and mix. Stir corn flakes and coconut into melted chocolate mixture.

Drop tablespoons on a parchment-lined cookie sheet and place in the refrigerator for 2 hours or until set.

Makes about 3 dozen cookies.

International Flavours

Canada is often described as a rich mix of divergent cultures that have retained their own identity — not just for one generation, but for many. Certainly new Canadians become Canadian, but at the same time, they often preserve their language, love of homeland, and customs.

So, too, our culinary traditions are fused with the traditions of countries around the globe. This chapter celebrates just a few of the countries that have contributed to our national identity: Switzerland, Italy, Germany, Greece, India, and Asia are all visited in these pages, but I have barely scratched the surface. An entire book could easily be devoted to the international flavour of Canadian cookies.

Swiss Anise Christmas Cookies

This recipe comes from Franz Walpert, the co-ordinator of the School of Hospitality and Tourism at Cambrian College of Applied Arts and Technology in Sudbury, Ontario. "Here is a cookie recipe from Switzerland, my home country. I still remember the smell that filled our kitchen every Christmas. Mom was busy baking a variety of Christmas cookies, which we enjoyed over the festive season."

2	eggs
1 1/4 cups (300ml)	sugar
1/4 cups plus 2 tbsp (75ml)	aniseed
2 1/4 cups (300ml)	pastry flour
Pinch	baking powder

Preheat oven to 300ºF (150ºC).

Spread 1/4 cup (50ml) aniseed on a cookie sheet and toast in oven until darkened and fragrant, about 3 to 5 minutes. Use a spice grinder or a mortar and pestle to grind until fine.

Cream together eggs and sugar until light and fluffy. In a separate bowl, mix together ground aniseed with flour and baking powder. Fold into egg mixture until a stiff dough forms. Let rest for 30 minutes.

Roll out dough between two sheets of plastic wrap to 1/2-inch (1cm) thickness. Cut out cookies with a 2-inch (5cm) cookie cutter and place on a greased cookie sheet. Chill in the refrigerator for 24 hrs to dry.

Preheat oven to 300ºF (150ºC).

Sprinkle remaining 2 tbsp (25ml) whole aniseed on cookies. Bake on the middle rack of the oven for 20 minutes. Do not brown. Keep cookies uncovered at room temperature for 24 hours to allow them to soften, then store in an air-tight container.

Makes about 2 dozen cookies.

Almond Pistachio Cookies

This cookie has a definite Italian flair, but pistachios are also native to California, Turkey and Iran, and can be found in the regional cuisines of these areas.

2/3 cup (150ml)	whole almonds
1/3 cup (75ml)	pistachios
1/2 cup (125ml)	sugar
1/3 cup (75ml)	cold butter, cubed
3/4 cup (175ml)	all-purpose flour
1/4 (1ml)	tsp salt
1 tsp (5ml)	minced orange zest
1	egg yolk

In a food processor, pulse almonds and pistachios with sugar until fine.

Add butter, flour, salt, and orange zest, and pulse until mixture resembles coarse meal. Transfer to a bowl and stir in egg yolk until a dough forms. Wrap in plastic and refrigerate for 2 hours.

Preheat oven to 350ºF (180ºC).

Roll out dough between two sheets of plastic wrap to 1/4-inch (5mm) thickness. Cut out 2-inch (5cm) cookies, any shape, and place on a greased baking sheet.

Bake in the middle rack of the oven for 8 to 10 minutes or until golden. Transfer to a rack to cool.

Makes about 2 dozen cookies.

Cardamom Cookies

Cardamom is a pungent spice that is native to India but also found in Scandinavian cooking. These aromatic cookies are best made with freshly ground cardamom.

1 cup (250ml)	flour
1/4 tsp (1ml)	baking powder
1/2 tsp (2ml)	ground cardamom
1/4 tsp (1ml)	ground cinnamon
1/4 tsp (1ml)	salt
1/3 cup (75ml)	cold butter, cubed
1/2 cup (125ml)	sugar
1/4 cup (50ml)	ground almonds
1 tsp (5ml)	grated lemon zest
1	egg, beaten
1 tsp (5ml)	vanilla

Preheat oven to 375ºF (190ºC).

In a medium bowl, mix together flour, baking powder, cardamom, cinnamon, and salt. Rub butter into flour until texture is coarse and mealy. Stir in sugar, almonds, and lemon zest. Make a well in the flour mixture and add egg and vanilla. Stir until mixed.

On a well-floured surface, press out dough to a 1/4-inch (5mm) thickness. Cut out cookies with 1-inch (2.5cm) cutters and place 1 inch (5cm) apart on a parchment-lined cookie sheet.

Bake for 8 to 10 minutes or until golden.

Makes about 3 dozen cookies.

Cardamom Vanilla Cookies

Green cardamom is most suited to use in baking, while brown or black cardamom is used in savoury cooking.

1 cup (250ml)	soft butter
1 cup (250ml)	sugar
2	eggs
1 tbsp (15ml)	vanilla
2 tbsp (25ml)	cream or buttermilk
3 cups (750ml)	all-purpose flour
1 tsp (5ml)	baking soda
1 tsp (5ml)	ground cardamom
1/4 tsp (1ml)	salt
1 cup (250ml)	buttered almonds

Preheat oven to 350°F (180°C).

Cream together butter and sugar until light and fluffy. Beat in eggs, one at a time, then vanilla and cream.

In a separate bowl, mix together flour, baking soda, cardamom, and salt. Stir flour mixture into creamed butter in thirds. Fold in buttered almonds.

Roll dough into 1-inch (5cm) balls and place 2 inches (5cm) on a parchment-lined cookie sheet. Flatten balls with the bottom of a glass dipped in sugar.

Bake on the middle rack of the oven for 12 to 15 minutes or until golden. Transfer to cooling racks.

Makes about 4 dozen cookies.

Orange Thyme Cookies

Thyme honey from Greece is a pure delight. If you happen to have a jar,
drizzle a little over these cookies for extra sweetness.

1 cup (250ml)	soft butter
1 cup (250ml)	sugar
2 tbsp (25ml)	honey
1	egg
1 tsp (5ml)	vanilla
1 tsp (5ml)	lemon juice
2 cups (500ml)	all-purpose flour
1/2 tsp (2ml)	baking soda
1/4 tsp (1ml)	salt
1 tbsp (15ml)	grated orange zest
1 tbsp (15ml)	fresh thyme, chopped
2 tbsp (25ml)	orange decorators' sugar
1	egg white, slightly beaten

Cream together butter and sugar until light and fluffy. Beat in honey, egg, vanilla, and lemon juice. In a separate bowl, mix together flour, baking soda and salt. Stir in orange zest and thyme.

Stir flour mixture into creamed butter in thirds. Roll dough into a log 1 1/2 inches (4cm) in diameter. Wrap in plastic or parchment and refrigerate for 2 hours.

Preheat oven to 375ºF (190ºC).

Brush log with egg white, then roll in orange decorators' sugar to cover. Cut into 1/2-inch (1cm) slices and place 2 inches (5cm) apart on a parchment-lined cookie sheet.

Bake on the middle rack of the oven for 12 to 14 minutes or until edges are golden. Transfer to cooling sheet.

Makes about 3 dozen cookies.

Lebkuchen

This traditional German cookie benefits from bright citrus tones.
Fresh nutmeg is always preferable to the pre-ground variety. Whole nutmeg
is sold in most supermarkets and a small grater is all that is needed.

1/2 cup (125ml)	soft butter	1/4 tsp (1ml)	ground cloves
1/2 cup (125ml)	packed brown sugar	1/4 tsp (1ml)	baking soda
1/4 cup (50ml)	honey	1/4 tsp (1ml)	salt
1	egg	1 tbsp (15ml)	grated lemon zest
2 cups (500ml)	all-purpose flour	1 tbsp (15ml)	grated orange zest
1 tsp (5ml)	nutmeg, freshly grated	2/3 cup (150ml)	powdered sugar
1 tsp (5ml)	cinnamon	2 tbsp (25ml)	orange juice
1/2 tsp (2ml)	ground ginger		

Cream together butter and sugar until light and fluffy. Beat in honey and egg.

In a separate bowl, combine flour, nutmeg, cinnamon, ginger, cloves, baking soda, salt, lemon zest, and orange zest. Stir flour mixture into creamed mixture in thirds. Refrigerate for 2 hours.

Roll out dough between 2 sheets of plastic wrap or waxed paper to 1/2-inch (1cm) thickness. Refrigerate overnight.

Preheat oven to 350ºF (180ºC).

On a lightly-floured surface, roll out dough to 1/4-inch (5mm) thickness and cut into 1x2-inch (2.5x5cm) bars. Place bars on a parchment-lined cookie sheet.

Bake on the middle rack of the oven for 10 to 12 minutes or until firm. Transfer to cooling racks. Stir together powdered sugar and orange juice until smooth and use to glaze the cookies.

Makes about 4 dozen cookies.

Amaretti

This Italian specialty is much like a meringue cookie. The name comes from the sweet almonds baked into this crisp macaroon.

1 1/4 cups (300ml)	ground almonds
3/4 cup (175ml)	powdered sugar
1 tsp (5ml)	all-purpose flour
2	egg whites
Pinch	cream of tartar
1/3 cup (75ml)	sugar
3/4 tsp (4ml)	lemon extract

Preheat oven to 300°F (150°C).

Mix together almonds, sugar, and flour.

In a clean glass, copper-lined or stainless steel bowl, beat egg whites with cream of tartar on low speed until they begin to hold their shape. Increase speed to medium and beat in sugar. Continue to beat until stiff peaks form. Fold in almond mixture and lemon extract.

Drop half tablespoons of dough 2 inches (5cm) apart on a greased parchment-lined cookie sheet.

Bake on the middle rack of the oven for 20 minutes or until golden.

Makes about 3 dozen cookies.

Lemon Grass Cookies

The blending of cultures in cuisine — often referred to as "fusion" — is here to stay. Asian flavours have been influencing Canadian tastes for some time, but over the last ten years our passion for exotic ingredients has played a major role in shaping modern cuisine. Use only the tender, inside leaves of the lemon grass stalk.

2/3 cup (150ml)	soft butter
2/3 cup (150ml)	sugar
1	egg
2 cup (500ml)	all-purpose flour
1 tsp (5ml)	baking powder
1 tsp (5ml)	ground ginger
1/4 tsp (1ml)	salt
1 tbsp (15ml)	lemon zest, minced
1 tbsp (15ml)	lemon grass, minced

Preheat oven to 350°F (180°C).

Cream together butter and sugar until light and creamy. Beat in egg.

In a separate bowl, combine flour, baking powder, ginger, and salt. Mix in lemon zest and lemon grass. Stir flour mixture into creamed mixture in thirds.

Form into 1-inch (2.5cm) balls and place 2 inches (5cm) apart on a parchment-lined cookie sheet. With a fork, make a crisscross pattern on the top of each cookie.

Bake on the middle rack of the oven for 12 to 15 minutes or until the edges are golden. Cool on cookie sheets for 2 minutes, then transfer to racks.

Makes about 2 dozen cookies.

Pistachio Phyllo Spirals

Phyllo pastry is a wonderful boon to the home cook. You can produce impressive desserts and pastries without sifting as much as a tablespoon of flour. Remember to keep the phyllo covered while you are working with it, and handle it with care — it is paper thin and tears easily.

6 sheets	phyllo pastry
1 tbsp (15ml)	melted butter
2 cups (500ml)	ground pistachio nuts
1/4 cup (50ml)	sugar
1/2 cup (125ml)	liquid honey

Preheat oven to 325°F (170°C).

Lay out one sheet of phyllo and lightly brush with melted butter. Place second sheet of pastry directly over the first and lightly brush with butter. Place third sheet directly over the second.

Combine ground pistachios and sugar. Sprinkle half the pistachio mixture over the pastry, leaving a 2-inch (5cm) strip at one end bare. Brush the bare end with butter then, starting at the opposite end, roll up the pastry like a jelly roll and seal the buttered edge. Cover with a slightly damp kitchen towel while preparing second roll with the remaining ingredients.

Using a serrated knife, cut the rolls into 3/4-inch (2cm) slices. Arrange 1 inch (2.5cm) apart on a parchment-lined cookie tray. Drizzle with honey.

Bake on the middle rack of the oven for 8 to 12 minutes or until golden.

Makes about 30 spirals.

Pastry Chefs and Bakers

A book on Canadian cookies could not be written without acknowledging the creative men and women working on the front lines of the baking industry. Pastry chefs and bakers in bakeries, restaurants, and hotels work hard to keep us in whipped cream and petit fours. We see the delicate beauty of the end product — the pastries, the wedding cakes, the breads and the scones — but not the long hours spent, often before the rest of us are awake, at industrial-sized mixers or banks of hot ovens.

I have always had tremendous respect for bakers and pastry chefs and it is with great happiness that I have seen them become an integral part of good restaurant food. Twenty years ago, most restaurants bought commercial breads and desserts. Now many of the better establishments make everything fresh, in-house, and the difference in quality is easily tasted. On the following pages you will find cookie recipes ranging from short bread to biscotti, created by these hard working professionals, and each one is terrific.

Ginger-Glazed Shortbread

Pastry chef Stefanie Killen writes, "This is a recipe I learned when I was in London and going to school at the Cordon Bleu. The addition of ginger gives a nice twist to traditional shortbread."

BISCUIT DOUGH

2 cups (500ml)	all-purpose flour
1/3 cup (75ml)	sugar
1 1/2 tsp (7ml)	ground ginger
1/2 tsp (2ml)	ground white pepper
3/4 cup plus 1 tbsp (190ml)	soft butter

GLAZE

1 tbsp (15ml)	corn syrup
1/4 cup (50ml)	butter
2 tbsp (25ml)	confectioners' sugar
2 tsp (10ml)	ground ginger

BISCUIT DOUGH

Preheat oven to 350ºF (180ºC).

Combine flour, sugar, ginger, and pepper Mix butter into flour until dough is crumbly and beginning to stick together. Press dough into an 11x7-inch (2L) oblong or 8-inch (2L) square pan.

Bake for approximately 30 minutes. The shortbread should be lightly browned.

GLAZE

Combine the syrup and butter in a small pan and warm over low heat until melted. Whisk in sugar and ginger. Pour warm glaze over shortbread while it is still warm. Cool slightly, then cut into 16 pieces

Makes about 16 cookies.

Coconut Macaroons

There have been many pastry chefs at the Senator Restaurant, but over the years Anne Hollyer has always managed this arena with talent and creativity. This was my favourite of the restaurant's many cookies.

1 1/4 cups (300ml)	all-purpose flour
1 1/3 cups (325ml)	sugar
1/2 tsp (2ml)	salt
5 cups (1.25L)	shredded coconut
1 1/4 cups (300ml)	egg whites (about 8 or 9)
2 tsp (10ml)	vanilla
1 cup (250ml)	semi-sweet chocolate chunks

Preheat oven to 325°F (160°C).

Stir together flour, sugar, and salt. Mix in coconut. Whip egg whites until stiff, then beat in vanilla. Fold in dry ingredients. Using a two-tablespoon measure, scoop dough onto a greased parchment-lined cookie sheet.

Bake on the middle rack of the oven for 17 to 20 minutes or until golden. Let cool on racks.

Melt chocolate in a bowl over hot (not boiling) water. When cookies have cooled, dip the flat bottom of each cookie in the chocolate. Let the chocolate harden (about 30 seconds) then return to the cooling rack. Use the remaining chocolate to drizzle line patterns over the top of the cookies.

Makes about 12 large macaroons.

Almond Macaroons

Here is my recipe for a smaller, more conventional almond macaroon.

4	egg whites
Pinch	cream of tartar
3/4 cup (175 ml)	almond paste
1 cup (250ml)	confectioners' sugar
Pinch	salt
2 tbsp (25ml)	ground almonds

Preheat oven to 300ºF (150ºC).

In a clean stainless steel, glass, or copper-lined bowl, beat egg whites with cream of tartar on low speed until they begin to hold their shape. Increase the speed to medium high and continue to beat until stiff peaks form.

In a separate bowl, mix together almond paste, sugar, and salt. Beat one third of the beaten egg whites into the almond paste, then fold in the remainder.

Drop heaping half-tablespoons of dough 1 inch (2.5cm) apart on greased parchment paper lining a cookie sheet. Sprinkle ground almonds over top.

Bake on the middle rack of the oven for 20 minutes or until golden. Turn off heat and leave macaroons in the oven with the door slightly ajar for an additional 15 minutes.

Makes about 2 dozen small macaroons.

Oat Macaroons

This oat macaroon was featured at a small B&B we enjoyed one weekend in Collingwood, Ontario. The baker was too busy to write down the recipe, but quickly dictated it to me. I wrote it on a napkin and reconstructed it when I got home.

1 tbsp (15ml)	melted shortening
1 cup (250ml)	sugar
4	eggs, separated
1 tsp (5ml)	vanilla
1 tsp (5ml)	almond extract
2 cups (500ml)	quick-cooking oats
1/2 cup (125ml)	shredded coconut
1 tsp (5ml)	baking powder
1/4 tsp (1ml)	salt
Pinch	cream of tartar

Preheat oven to 325°F (170°C).

Cream together shortening and sugar, then beat in egg yolks, vanilla, and almond extract. In a separate bowl, combine oats, coconut, baking powder, and salt. Stir into creamed mixture in thirds.

In a clean stainless steel, glass, or copper-lined bowl, beat egg whites with cream of tartar on low speed until they begin to hold their shape. Increase speed to medium high and beat until stiff peaks form. Fold oat mixture into beaten egg whites. Drop teaspoons of dough 2 inches (5cm) apart on greased parchment paper lining a cookie sheet.

Bake on the middle rack of the oven for 10 minutes or until golden. Transfer to cooling racks.

Makes about 6 dozen small macaroons.

Chocolate Orange Shortbread

Here's another favourite from Toronto's Senator Restaurant. I love the appearance of this cookie — orange speckles and a large chunk of chocolate in the centre.

1 cup (250ml)	soft butter
2/3 cup (150ml)	sugar
1 1/3 cups (325ml)	pastry flour
2/3 cup (150ml)	all-purpose flour
1/2 tsp (2ml)	salt
Zest from 12	oranges
1 cup (250ml)	semi-sweet chocolate chunks
20	large chocolate chunks (for decorating)

Preheat oven to 325°F (160°C).

Cream together butter and sugar until light and fluffy. Sift together flours and salt. Stir in zest.

Stir flour mixture into creamed butter, and mix in chocolate chunks. Roll cookies into 2-inch (5cm) balls. Flatten slightly, and place a large chocolate chunk firmly in the centre of each cookie.

Bake on the middle rack of the oven for 15 to 18 minutes or until edges are golden.

Makes about 20 cookies.

Triple-Chocolate Biscotti

*This recipe comes from the files of pastry chef Stefanie Killen,
and it also appeared in my book, Nice Timing.*

1/2 cup (125ml)	soft butter
1 3/4 cups (425ml)	brown sugar
2	eggs
2 1/2 cups (625ml)	whole almonds
1/2 cup (125ml)	chopped dark chocolate
1/2 cup (125ml)	chopped milk chocolate
1/2 cup (125ml)	chopped white chocolate
2 1/2 cups (625ml)	all-purpose flour
1/2 tsp (2ml)	baking powder

Preheat oven to 350°F (180°C).

Cream butter and sugar until light and fluffy. Beat in eggs, one at a time. Stir in almonds and chocolate. Sift together flour and baking powder. Fold into wet ingredients until just incorporated.

Divide the dough into two equal-sized pieces and shape into two logs about 2 inches (5cm) in diameter and the length of the cookie sheet. Place logs on a parchment-lined cookie sheet.

Bake for 15 to 20 minutes or until golden brown.

Reduce oven temperature to 325°F (160°C).

Cool for 10 minutes. While still warm, slice each log into 10 cookies. Lay biscotti on cookie sheet and bake for 10 to 15 minutes.

Cool, then store in an airtight container for up to three weeks.

Makes about 12 biscotti.

Sablés normands au chocolat

*This contribution is from Sandra MacInnis of Le Cordon Bleu
Culinary Arts Institute in Ottawa. I was thrilled to be able to include
a recipe from one of Canada's première culinary institutes.*

3 1/2 oz (100g)	icing sugar	1	egg
3 1/2 oz (100g)	almond powder	1 tsp (5ml)	milk
7 oz (200g)	soft butter	2 oz (50g)	dried fruit and nuts
3 1/2 oz (100g)	icing sugar (sieved)		(chopped almonds,
Pinch	salt		pistachios, and hazelnuts)
2 oz (60g)	egg yolks	3 oz (75g)	dark chocolate
1/4 oz (10g)	vanilla sugar		
9 oz (250g)	flour, sieved		
1/2 oz (15g)	cocoa powder		

Mix together 3 1/2 oz (100g) icing sugar and almond powder.

In a separate bowl, cream together butter and sieved icing sugar. Add salt, almond powder mixture, egg yolks, and vanilla sugar. Add the sieved flour and the cocoa powder. Chill dough in refrigerator for at least 2 hours.

Preheat oven to 375°F (190°C).

On a lightly-floured surface, roll out the dough to 1/4-inch (5mm) thickness. Beat milk into egg and brush over dough. Cover dough with dried fruit and nuts. Cut into desired shapes with cookie-cutter. Place pieces 1 inch (2.5cm) on a parchment-lined cookie sheet.

Bake on the middle rack of the oven for 10 minutes or until edges are golden. Transfer to cooling racks.

Melt chocolate in double boiler or stainless steel bowl, over hot (not boiling) water. Dip cooled cookies in the chocolate.

Makes 2 to 4 dozen cookies (depending on size).

Chocolate Lady Fingers

My husband cooked for a time at Benjamin's Inn in the picturesque village of St. Jacobs. While there he had the opportunity to work with Melissa Smith, a talented young pastry chef. The following three recipes come from Melissa's repetoire. Pastry chefs measure the ingredients by weight rather than by volume because this method is more accurate.

2 oz (50g)	cornstarch
1 oz (25g)	cocoa powder
4 oz (125g)	bread flour
6	eggs, separated
6 oz (175g)	sugar
1/2 tsp (2ml)	lemon juice

Preheat oven to 425°F (220°C).

Sift cornstarch, cocoa, and cocoa together.

Whip egg yolks with 2 oz (50g) sugar until light and creamy. Whip egg whites with lemon juice and 2 oz (50g) sugar. Add remaining sugar to whites and whip until stiff peaks form.

Fold yolk mixture into white mixture, then fold in flour mix.

Put dough into a piping bag with a large, plain tube. Pipe 2-inch (5cm) lengths onto a parchment-lined cookie sheet.

Bake on the middle rack of the oven for 10 minutes or until set. Transfer to cooling racks.

Makes 2 dozen cookies.

Hazelnut and Crème-de-Cacao Fingers

*This recipe, created by Melissa Smith, is similar to my recipe for
Chocolate-Dipped Hazelnut Fingers on p. 174. Here we have a prime example
of how two cooks can take similar ingredients and produce quite different results.
The effect of the crème de cacao in Melissa's cookies is fantastic.*

1/3 cup (75ml)	chopped hazelnuts
3/4 cup (175ml)	soft butter
4 1/2 tbsp (60ml)	sugar
1 tbsp (15ml)	crème de cacao
1/2 tsp (2ml)	vanilla
1 1/2 cups (375ml)	all-purpose flour
1/4 tsp (1ml)	salt
2 1/4 oz (65g)	dark chocolate, grated
4 oz (125g)	semisweet chocolate
2 tbsp (25ml)	icing sugar (for garnish)

Preheat oven to 325°F (160°C).

Spread hazelnuts out on a baking tray and roast for 10 to 12 minutes. Remove skins and chop finely in a food processor.

Cream together butter and sugar until light and fluffy. Beat in liqueur and vanilla. In a separate bowl, combine flour and salt. Stir flour mixture into creamed mixture in thirds. Fold in nuts and grated chocolate.

Shape dough into 3-inch (8cm) crescents and place 2 inches (5cm) apart on a parchment-lined cookie sheet.

Bake on the middle rack of the oven for 20 to 25 minutes or until golden. Transfer to cooling racks.

In a double boiler or stainless steel bowl over hot (not boiling) water, melt the chocolate. Dip cooled cookies halfway into chocolate to coat. Return to cooling rack. Sprinkle the plain half of each crescent with icing sugar.

Makes about 2 dozen cookies.

Christmas Cookies

At no other time during the year is cookie production more furious than during the holidays. For me, holiday cookies always bring back memories of my grandmother, and I can see her now, starting her Christmas baking. The cookies began making their appearance in mid-October and we would be treated to an update of her cookie count at every visit. Hundreds of dozens of cookies in every conceivable form or fashion were frozen, put in tins, or wrapped and sent off to distant relatives for the upcoming festivities. Of course, there were always a few extras in each batch for hungry little helpers!

Many people save their fanciest cookies for Christmas, so this chapter is replete with spirals, pinwheels, wreaths, and other intricate delicacies. And finally, there is gingerbread. What holiday season would be complete without decorating little gingerbread people or assembling a house festooned with candy and gobs of sticky icing. More than anything else, Christmas is a time to celebrate the family and to bask in the warmth of love and generosity. I hope some of these cookies will be welcomed at your family table this holiday season.

figgy Spirals

Forget the figgy pudding — these pinwheel treats will bring the marvelous taste of fresh figs to your Christmas cookie collection.

3/4 cup (175ml)	soft butter
1 cup (250ml)	sugar
2	egg yolks
1/2 tsp (2ml)	vanilla
1/4 cup (50ml)	ground almonds
1 1/4 cups (300ml)	all-purpose flour
1 cup (250ml)	ground oats
1/2 tsp (2ml)	salt
1/2 cup (125ml)	apple butter
6	fresh figs

Cream together butter and sugar until light and fluffy. Beat in yolks and vanilla. In a separate bowl, combine ground almonds, flour, oats, and salt. Stir flour mixture into creamed mixture in thirds.

Roll out dough between sheets of plastic wrap or waxed paper into 2 rectangular sheets, 1/8 inch (3mm) thick.

Spread one third of the apple butter over the surface of each sheet, leaving 1/4 inch (5mm) bare around the edges. Cut figs into thin slices and layer over apple butter. Roll up like a jelly roll and freeze for 30 minutes.

Preheat oven to 375ºF (190ºC).

Cut each roll into 1/2-inch (1cm) slices and place 1 inch (2.5cm) apart on a parchment-lined cookie sheet.

Bake on the middle rack of the oven for 11 to 13 minutes or until golden. Transfer to cooling racks.

Makes about 3 dozen pinwheels.

Greek Melomacarona

This recipe was given to me years ago by a waitress. Olive oil and beer may seem an odd mix in a Christmas cookie, but the test is in the tasting.

1/4 cup (50ml)	soft butter
1/2 cup (125ml)	sugar
3/4 cups (175ml)	olive oil
1/2 cup (125ml)	beer
4 cups (1L)	all-purpose flour
1 tbsp (15ml)	grated orange zest
1 tsp (5ml)	cinnamon
1/2 tsp (2ml)	baking powder
1/2 tsp (2ml)	baking soda
1/4 tsp (1ml)	salt
1/4 tsp (1ml)	ground cloves

SYRUP

1 cup (250ml)	sugar
1 cup (250ml)	honey
1/2 cup (125ml)	water
1/4 cup (50ml)	chopped walnuts

Preheat oven to 350ºF (180ºC).

Cream together butter and sugar until light and fluffy. Beat in olive oil and beer. In a separate bowl, mix together flour, orange zest, cinnamon, baking powder, baking soda, salt and cloves. Stir flour mixture into wet ingredients in thirds.

Roll dough into cigar shapes, 2 inches (3cm) long, and flatten slightly. Place 2 inches (5cm) apart on greased cookie sheets.

Bake on the middle rack of the oven for 27 to 30 minutes or until the cookies are golden at the edges and dry. Transfer to cooling racks.

In a medium-sized, nonreactive pan, combine sugar, honey, and water. Simmer for 3 to 5 minutes or until the syrup coats the back of a spoon.

Set cooled cookies to a shallow dish. Pour syrup over the tops and dust with walnuts. Let cookies sit overnight to absorb the syrup.

Makes about 3 dozen cookies.

Gingerbread People

If you are using this recipe for a gingerbread house, knead the dough in order to work the gluten. This will provide a sturdier cookie for building walls. Roll dough into sheets and cut the necessary pieces for constructing the house. Make a paper pattern of the house first and put it together to make sure it works. You can often find ginger-bread-house patterns in the Christmas cookie sections of magazines or cookbooks.

1/3 cup (75ml)	brown sugar, packed
1/3 cup (75ml)	shortening, softened
2/3 cups (150ml)	molasses
1	egg
2 3/4 cups (675ml)	flour
1 tsp (5ml)	baking powder
1 tsp (5ml)	ground ginger
1/4 tsp (1ml)	salt

Cream together sugar and shortening until soft and fluffy. Beat in molasses and egg.

In a separate bowl, mix together flour, baking powder, ginger, and salt. Stir flour mixture into shortening mixture in thirds. Knead dough for 3 minutes. Refrigerate for 1 hour.

Preheat oven to 375ºF (190ºC).

On a lightly-floured surface, roll the dough out to 1/4-inch (5mm) thickness. Use cookie cutters to cut out shapes of people or seasonal objects.

Place 2 inches (5cm) apart on a greased cookie sheet.

Bake on the middle rack of the oven for 10 to 12 minutes or until browned on bottom. Transfer to cooling racks.

When cool, use decorators' icing to give the cookies your own personal touch.

Makes about 12 large or 30 small gingerbread people.

Decorators' Icing

Several recipes in the book call for this icing.
Use the appropriate food colouring to obtain the desired colour.

1	egg white
1 1/2 cups (375ml)	confectioners' sugar
1 tsp (5ml)	vanilla
	Food colouring as needed

In a small bowl, slowly whip the sugar into the egg white until the texture is thick enough to pipe. Stir in vanilla. Add food colouring, one drop at a time, until the colour suits.

Spoon icing into a small piping bag and use to decorate cookies.

Makes 1/2 cup (125ml).

Noël Wreaths

These festive cookies were contributed by Marjorie McGee
of Montague, Prince Edward Island, via The Guardian.

1 cup (250ml)	soft butter
1/2 cup (125ml)	sugar
1	egg
1 tsp (5ml)	vanilla
2 1/4 cups (550ml)	flour
1 cup (250ml)	finely chopped walnuts
1/4 cup (50ml)	corn syrup
1/4 tsp (1ml)	maple flavouring
1/4 cup (50ml)	candied red and green cherries

Preheat oven to 350ºF (180ºC).

Cream together butter and sugar until light and fluffy. Beat in egg and vanilla. Sift in flour, folding until a soft dough forms.

In a separate bowl, measure out 1/4 cup (50ml) of dough and mix with walnuts, corn syrup, and maple flavouring.

Fit a star-shaped plate on a cookie press and fill with remaining dough. Press out dough into 4-inch (10cm) lengths on an ungreased cookie sheet. Join the ends of each length to form a small circle. Fill the centre of each circle with a 1 tsp (5ml) of the syrup nut mixture. Flatten cherries, cut out small triangles, and arrange two triangles on each cookie to form festive bows.

Bake on the middle rack of the oven for 12 to15 minutes or until golden. Transfer to wire rack to cool. Store in an airtight container with wax paper between layers.

Makes about 4 dozen cookies.

Mincemeat Pillows

The Island Christmas Web site hosted by The Guardian has dozens of recipes for genuine Prince Edward Island cookies. This one was submitted by Bob Simmons of Montague, P.E.I.

1 cup (250ml)	soft butter
1 1/2 cups (375ml)	sugar
2	eggs
1/2 cup (125ml)	milk
1 tsp (5ml)	vanilla
3 1/2 cups (875ml)	all-purpose flour
1 tsp (5ml)	baking soda
1/2 tsp (2ml)	salt
1 jar (8 oz/237ml)	mincemeat

Preheat oven to 350°F (180°C).

Cream together butter and sugar until light and fluffy. Beat in eggs, one at a time, followed by milk and vanilla. In a separate bowl, stir together flour, baking soda and salt. Stir into creamed butter in thirds.

Roll out dough on a lightly-floured surface to 1/8-inch (3mm) thickness. Cut into 2 1/2-inch (6cm) circles and place on a greased baking sheet.

Drop 2 tsp (10ml) of mincemeat into the centre of half the circles. Cover with a second circle. Press edges closed with a floured fork or fingertips. Make two 1/2-inch (1cm) vents on the top of each pillow to allow steam to escape. Brush egg wash over each pillow and sprinkle with additional sugar.

Bake on the middle rack of the oven for 10 minutes or until lightly browned.

Makes about 4 dozen cookies.

Date Applesauce Cookies

Our family friend Gary Reiner happily cooked many of our holiday
meals for years. A consummate host, he baked breads and also these cookies.
For variation, substitute chocolate chips for the dates.

1 3/4 cup (425ml)	quick-cooking oats
1 1/2 cups (375ml)	all-purpose flour
1 tsp (5ml)	salt
1 tsp (5ml)	baking powder
1/2 tsp (2ml)	baking soda
1 tsp (5ml)	cinnamon
1/2 cup (125ml)	soft butter
1 cup (250ml)	firmly packed brown sugar
1/2 cup (125ml)	granulated sugar
1	large egg
3/4 cup (175ml)	apple sauce
3/4 cup (175ml)	finely chopped dates

Preheat oven to 350ºF (180ºC).

Combine oats, flour, salt, baking powder, baking soda, and cinnamon in a bowl and set aside.

In a large bowl, cream butter and sugars, then beat in egg. Gradually stir in the flour mixture and the apple sauce, alternating in thirds. Stir in dates. Drop level tablespoons of dough on a greased cookie sheet

Bake on middle rack of oven for 15 minutes or until golden.

Makes about 3 dozen cookies.

Brown Sugar Rings

*This cookie is prepared like a pastry — the butter
is rubbed into the flour rather than creamed with the sugar.
The result is a delicate dough formed into attractive rings.*

1 cup (250ml)	all-purpose flour
2 tbps (25ml)	cocoa powder
2 tsp (10ml)	cinnamon
1/2 tsp (2ml)	freshly ground nutmeg
Pinch	salt
3/4 cup (175ml)	cold butter
3/4 cup (175ml)	ground almonds
1/4 cup (50ml)	tightly packed brown sugar
1 tsp (5ml)	vanilla

Preheat oven to 325°F (160°C).

Sift together flour, cocoa, cinnamon, nutmeg, and salt. Cut butter into small pieces and rub into flour mixture until the texture resembles coarse meal. Stir in almonds, sugar, and vanilla until dough comes together.

Roll dough into ropes 1/2 inch (1cm) thick, and cut each rope into 3-inch (8cm) segments. Form each segment into a circle and twist the ends together. Place circles 1 inch (2.5cm) apart on an ungreased cookie sheet.

Bake on the middle rack of the oven for 12 to 15 minutes or until firm. Cool on cookie sheets for 2 minutes, then transfer to racks.

Makes about 12 rings.

Date Oatmeal Cookies

Of all my Grandma Gladys' many incredible cookies, these are my favourite.
This recipe appeared in Recipes for Homemade Love, my tribute to our
grandmothers' fine cooking. Whenever I go anywhere to promote my books,
I bring a big batch of these cookies and I am received with open arms.

1 cup (250ml)	granulated sugar
1 cup (250ml)	brown sugar
1 cup (250ml)	soft butter
2	eggs
1/4 cup (50ml)	35% cream
1 tsp (5ml)	vanilla
2 cups (500ml)	all-purpose flour
1 tsp (5ml)	cinnamon
1 tsp (5ml)	baking powder
1/2 tsp (2ml)	baking soda
1/2 tsp (2ml)	salt
2 1/4 cups (550ml)	quick-cooking oats
1/2 cup (125ml)	chopped dates

Preheat oven to 350ºF (180ºC).

Cream together sugars and butter. Beat in eggs, cream and vanilla.

Sift together flour, cinnamon, baking powder, baking soda and salt, and stir in oats and dates. Fold dry ingredients into creamed mixture. Refrigerate for 1 hour.

Roll dough into 1-inch (2.5cm) balls and place 1 inch (2.5cm) apart on an ungreased cookie sheet. Do not flatten.

Bake for 7 to 10 minutes or until edges are darkened.

Makes about 8 dozen cookies.

Simple Christmas Cookies

This basic cookie is often the first to be eaten from a Christmas tray. In times of opulence, a little simplicity is often welcome.

1 cup (250ml)	soft butter
2/3 cup (150ml)	sugar
2	eggs
1 tsp (5ml)	vanilla
2 cups (500ml)	sifted all-purpose flour
1/2 tsp (2ml)	baking powder
1/4 tsp (1ml)	salt
1 tbsp (15ml)	coloured sugar

Preheat oven to 350°F (180°C).

Cream together butter and sugar until light and fluffy. Beat in eggs, one at a time, then vanilla.

Mix together flour, baking powder and salt. Stir flour mixture into creamed butter in thirds.

Spoon dough into a cookie gun and press out seasonal shapes on a parchment-lined cookie sheet. Sprinkle cookies with coloured sugar.

Bake on the middle rack of the oven for 12 to 15 minutes or until edges are darkened. Transfer to cooling racks.

Makes about 4 dozen cookies.

Christmas Pinwheels

Festive red and green decorators' sugar is a popular addition to many seasonal cookies. Chilling the dough makes it easier to cut. (Dough at room temperature would be too soft and the logs would not keep their shape.)

1 cup (250ml)	soft butter
1 1/2 cups (375ml)	sugar
1 tsp (5ml)	vanilla
1/2 cup (125ml)	sour cream
2 cups (500ml)	all-purpose flour
1/4 tsp (1ml)	salt
3 tbsp (50ml)	red sugar
3 tbsp (50ml)	green sugar

Cream together butter and sugar until light and fluffy. Beat in vanilla and sour cream. In a separate bowl, mix together flour and salt. Stir flour mixture into creamed mixture in thirds. Divide dough into 2 equal portions.

Between two sheets of waxed paper, roll out each portion of dough into a square 1/4 inch (5mm) thick. Sprinkle red sugar over one square and green sugar over the other. Roll each square into a log and refrigerate for 1 hour.

Preheat oven to 350ºF (180ºC).

Cut chilled dough into 1/2-inch (1cm) slices and place 1 inch (2.5cm) apart on a greased baking sheet.

Bake for 13 to 16 minutes or until edges are golden. Transfer to cooling racks.

Makes about 3 dozen cookies.

Chocolate Bourbon Balls

These liquor-soaked morsels are ideal for kicking off the festive season.

1 cup (250ml)	powdered sugar
2 tbsp (25ml)	cocoa
1/4 cup (50ml)	bourbon
2 1/2 tbsp (40ml)	liquid honey
1 cup (250ml)	crushed almonds
1 cup (250ml)	crushed hazelnuts
1 1/2 cups (375ml)	graham cracker crumbs
1 cup (250ml)	semi-sweet chocolate
1/3 cup (75ml)	whipping cream

Sift together sugar and cocoa. In a separate bowl, whisk together bourbon and honey. Stir the bourbon mixture into the sugar. In another bowl, combine almonds, hazelnuts, and graham crumbs.

Stir the nut mixture into the liquid ingredients. Press dough into 1-inch (2.5cm) balls and place on a wire rack.

Melt chocolate in a double boiler or a stainless steel bowl over hot (not boiling) water. Stir in whipping cream. Pour or spoon chocolate over balls to coat and let chocolate cool to set.

Makes about 3 dozen balls.

Cinnamon Almond Cookies

*Creaming the butter and sugar together incorporates air into
the cookie dough and gives the cookie its light structure.*

2/3 cup (150ml)	soft butter
1 cup (250ml)	sugar
1	egg
1 tsp (5ml)	vanilla
1 1/3 cups (325ml)	all-purpose flour, sifted
1/2 cup (125ml)	ground almonds
1 tsp (5ml)	baking powder
1 tsp (5ml)	cinnamon
1/4 tsp (1ml)	salt
2 tsp (10ml)	cinnamon
2 tbsp (25ml)	sugar

Preheat oven to 350ºF (180ºC).

Cream butter and sugar until light and fluffy. Beat in egg and vanilla.

In a separate bowl, mix together flour, almonds, baking powder, 1 tsp (5ml) cinnamon, and salt. Stir flour mixture into creamed butter in thirds.

Combine 2 tbsp (25ml) cinnamon and sugar. Shape dough into 1-inch (2.5cm) balls and roll in cinnamon-sugar mixture to coat. Place 3 inches (8cm) apart on a greased cookie sheet.

Bake for 10 to 12 minutes or until golden. Transfer to cooling racks.

Makes about 4 dozen cookies.

Cinnamon Trees

All ingredients should be at room temperature when you begin baking. If the eggs are cold, place them (in their shells) in warm water for a couple of minutes.

1/4 cup (50ml)	soft butter
1 1/2 (375ml)	cups sugar
2	eggs
1	egg yolk
1 tsp (5ml)	lemon juice
3 cups (750ml)	all-purpose flour
1 tbsp (15ml)	cinnamon
2 tsp (10ml)	baking powder
1/4 tsp (1ml)	ground cloves
1/4 tsp (1ml)	freshly grated nutmeg
1/4 tsp (1ml)	salt
1/2 cup (125ml)	ground hazelnuts
1	egg white, slightly beaten
1/2 cup (125ml)	green decorators' sugar

Preheat oven to 375ºF (190ºC).

Cream together butter and sugar. Beat in eggs and egg yolk, one at a time, then lemon juice. In a separate bowl, mix together flour, cinnamon, baking powder, cloves, nutmeg, and salt. Stir into creamed mixture in thirds. Fold in hazelnuts.

Between 2 sheets of waxed paper, roll out dough to 1/4-inch (5mm) thickness. Cut out shapes with Christmas-tree cookie cutters and place 2 inches (5cm) apart on a parchment-lined cookie sheet. Brush with egg white and sprinkle green sugar over the top.

Bake on the middle rack of the oven for 10 minutes or until edges are darkened. Transfer to cooling racks.

Makes about 2 dozen cookies.

Meringue Kisses

For a decadent twist, beat 1 cup (250ml) of whipping cream until stiff and sandwich pairs of kisses together with 1 tbsp (15ml) of whipped cream.

2	egg whites
1/2 cup (125ml)	sugar
Pinch	cream of tartar
Pinch	salt
1/2 tsp (2ml)	vanilla
3/4 cup (175ml)	ground almonds
1 cup (250ml)	finely chopped dates

Preheat oven to 250°F (120°C).

In a clean stainless steel, glass or copper-lined bowl, beat egg whites on low speed until they begin to hold their shape. Increase speed to medium and gradually beat in sugar and cream of tartar. Increase speed to medium high and beat in salt and vanilla. Beat until stiff peaks form. Fold in almonds and dates.

Drop heaping teaspoons 2 inches (5cm) apart on a lightly-greased, parchment-lined cookie sheet.

Bake on the middle rack of the oven for 15 minutes. Turn, and bake for 15 minutes more. Turn heat off and leave kisses in oven for 30 minutes. Open the oven door and let them sit for 10 minutes more.

Makes about 3 dozen kisses.

Cashew Shortbread

The following three recipes come from the home economists of the Blue Flame Kitchen™ at ATCO Gas in Alberta, and are published in their cookbook, A Blue Flame Kitchen™ Holiday Collection.

1 3/4 cups (425ml)	all-purpose flour
1/2 tsp (2ml)	baking powder
1 cup (250ml)	soft butter
1/2 cup (125ml)	icing sugar
1 cup (250ml)	coarsely chopped salted cashews

Sift together flour and baking powder. In a separate bowl, cream together butter and icing sugar. Stir in flour mixture in thirds, then fold in cashews.

Shape dough into 2 logs, wrap in plastic, and refrigerate for 2 hours.

Preheat oven to 375ºF (190ºC).

Slice logs into 1/4-inch (5mm) pieces and place on an ungreased cookie sheet.

Bake on the middle rack of the oven for 15 minutes or until golden. Transfer to cooling racks.

Makes about 4 dozen cookies.

Yule Logs

*Hats off to The Blue Flame Kitchen™ for
coming up with this festive treat.*

1 cup (250ml)	soft butter	**BUTTER FROSTING**	
2 tsp (20ml)	vanilla	3 tbsp (50ml)	soft butter
2 tsp (10ml)	rum extract	1/2 tsp (2ml)	vanilla
3/4 cup (175ml)	sugar	1 tsp (5ml)	rum extract
1	egg	1 1/4 cups (300ml)	icing sugar
3 cups (750ml)	flour	1 tbsp (15ml)	light cream
1 tsp (5ml)	nutmeg		nutmeg (for garnish)

Preheat oven to 350°F (180°C).

Cream butter with vanilla and rum extract. Gradually beat in sugar, then egg. In a separate bowl, mix together flour and nutmeg. Stir into butter mixture in thirds.

Shape dough into long rolls 1/2 inch (1cm) in diameter. Cut rolls into 3-inch (8cm) lengths, and place 2 inches (5cm) apart on a greased cookie tray.

Bake on the middle rack of the oven for 12 to 15 minutes or until lightly browned. Transfer to cooling racks.

BUTTER FROSTING

Cream together butter, vanilla and rum extract. Blend in icing sugar and cream, and beat until smooth and creamy.

Frost the top and sides of the cooled cookies, and score cookies with the tines of a fork so that they resemble logs. Grate nutmeg over top to garnish.

Makes about 3 1/2 dozen cookies.

White Chocolate Brownies

These brownies are from A Blue Flame Kitchen™ Holiday Collection.
The white chocolate gives them a great taste and an unusual presentation.

1/3 cup (75ml)	soft butter
8 oz (230g)	white chocolate, chopped
1/2 cup (125ml)	sugar
2	eggs
1 1/2 tsp (7ml)	vanilla
1/2 cup (125ml)	flour
1/2 cup (125ml)	chopped pecans
1	SKOR™ bar, chopped

Preheat oven to 350°F (180°C).

Melt butter in a medium saucepan. Remove from heat and stir in 1 cup (250ml) of chopped chocolate until melted. Stir in sugar.

Beat in eggs, one at a time. (The mixture may appear to separate after the addition of the first egg, but it will become smooth with addition of the second egg.) Stir in vanilla and flour.

Spread dough into a greased 8-inch (2L) square pan. Sprinkle with remaining chocolate, pecans, and pieces of SKOR™ bar.

Bake on the middle rack of the oven for 35 minutes or until set. Transfer to a cooling rack. Once cool, cut into 2-inch (5cm) squares.

Makes 16 squares.

Cookies by Post

*The Blue Flame Kitchen™ offers the following tips for sending cookies by mail.**

Choose firm crisp cookies such as gingersnaps or sugar cookies for mailing. Fragile, tender cookies will tend to break and crumble. Soft cookies, such as hermits will go stale and may mold. Frosted cookies do not travel well.

A sturdy cardboard box is ideal for packing cookies. Line the box with foil or plastic wrap and place a cushioning layer of crumpled wax paper, paper towel or popped popcorn on the bottom.

Wrap two cookies at a time, bottoms together, in wax paper or plastic wrap. Place wrapped cookies, side by side, in a single layer on bottom. Layer remaining cookies on top with a cushioning between each layer. Fill any open spaces or corners with additional cushioning so there is no movement in the box.

Tape the lid securely to seal the edges, and wrap the box with strong brown paper. Mark the package "Fragile" and send it "First Class" to ensure the cookies arrive fresh and unbroken.

A Blue Flame Kitchen™ Holiday Collection: 75th Anniversary Commemorative Edition (ATCO Gas, 1998), p. 81.

Seasonal Cookies

Christmas is not the only time for baking. Every season brings with it festive appetites and an excellent excuse to spend some time in your kitchen. In fact, in North America, cookies were originally made only for festivals and holidays as a special treat. This chapter has suggestions for everything from Love Turtles for Valentine's day to elegant Lace Cookies for New Year's Eve.

Since holidays are tied to seasons, many of the cookies in this chapter reflect seasonal foods: Thanksgiving features cranberries and apples, spring is the time to enjoy fresh raspberries, and Halloween cookies are made with pumpkin seeds. Our lives are marked by these passing holidays, and cookies become a tradition in families. How better to remember the joys of time spent in the warmth of each other's company than with a cookie? I know that in years to come, whenever I bake Easter Egg Cookies, I will be transported back to the laughter and gaiety I enjoyed while decorating these cookies with my young son.

Love Turtles

*Ohhh, I love Turtles™. Why not bake them into a gooey delight
to share with your special someone on Valentine's day?*

1/2 cup (125ml)	soft butter
1/4 cup (50ml)	granulated sugar
1/4 cup (50ml)	brown sugar
1	egg
1 tsp (5ml)	vanilla
3 oz (75g)	semi-sweet chocolate
1 1/4 cups (300ml)	all-purpose flour
1 tsp (5ml)	baking powder
1/4 tsp (1ml)	salt
24	Turtles™

Preheat oven to 375ºF (190ºC).

Cream together butter and sugars until light and fluffy. Beat in egg and vanilla. Melt chocolate in a double boiler or stainless steel bowl over hot (not boiling) water. Stir chocolate into creamed mixture.

In a separate bowl, combine flour, baking powder, and salt. Stir flour mixture into chocolate mixture in thirds.

Roll dough into 1 1/2-inch (4cm) balls and place 3 inches (8cm) apart on a parchment-lined cookie sheet. Gently press one Turtle™ into the centre of each cookie.

Bake on the middle rack of the oven for 12 to 15 minutes or until bottoms are slightly darkened.

Makes about 10 large cookies.

Domino Cookies

This recipe will be easier to follow if you have a domino to use as a decorating guide. These cookies may seem strange for a Valentine theme, but my sweetie and I have a tradition of playing a game of cookie dominoes every year.

1 cup (250ml)	soft butter
1 cup (250ml)	sugar
1/4 cup (50ml)	milk
1	egg
1 tsp (5ml)	vanilla
2 cups (500ml)	all-purpose flour
1/4 cup (50ml)	cocoa
2 tsp (10ml)	baking powder
1 tsp (5ml)	cinnamon
1/4 tsp (1ml)	freshly grated nutmeg
1/2 cup (125ml)	white chocolate chips

Cream together butter and sugar until light and creamy. Beat in milk, egg, and vanilla.

In a separate bowl, combine flour, cocoa, baking powder, cinnamon, and nutmeg. Stir flour mixture into creamed mixture in thirds. Refrigerate dough for 1 hour.

Preheat oven to 350ºF (180ºC).

Working with half the dough at a time, on a lightly-floured surface, roll out dough to 1/4-inch (5mm) thickness. Cut into 1x2-inch (2.5x5cm) rectangles. Make a ridge across the middle of each rectangle to resemble the two halves of a domino stone, and press white chocolate chips, tip-down, in domino patterns. Place on a parchment-lined cookie sheet.

Bake on the middle rack of the oven for 10 to 12 minutes.

Makes about 3 dozen dominoes.

Lemon Poppy-Seed Cookies

The elation that bubbles in the hearts of Canadians with the coming of spring can only be understood if you have endured a long, dark Canadian winter. These bright little cookies are perfectly suited to a light, spring appetite.

1/3 cup (75ml)	soft butter			
1/4 cup (50ml)	sugar			
1/2 cup (125ml)	liquid honey			
2	eggs		**GLAZE**	
2 cups (500ml)	all-purpose flour		1 cup (250ml)	powdered sugar
2 tbsp (25ml)	poppy seeds		2 tbsp (25ml)	lemon juice
1 tbsp (15ml)	grated lemon zest		1 tbsp (15ml)	poppy seeds
1 tsp (5ml)	baking powder			
1/2 tsp (2ml)	baking soda			
Pinch	salt			

Preheat oven to 350ºF (180ºC).

Cream together butter and sugar until light and fluffy. Beat in honey, then eggs, one at a time. In a separate bowl, combine flour, poppy seeds, lemon peel, baking powder, baking soda, and salt.

Stir flour mixture into creamed mixture in thirds. Drop heaping teaspoons 2 inches (5cm) apart on a greased cookie sheet.

Bake on the middle rack of the oven for 7 to 9 minutes or until golden. Transfer to cooling racks.

Whisk together powdered sugar, and lemon juice. Drizzle glaze over cookies and dust with poppy seeds.

Makes about 4 dozen cookies.

Raspberry Velvet Tarts

This recipe is a variation on a dessert flan we made at Andre's Restaurant in Toronto's Cabbagetown. Scaled down, it makes an attractive cookie that is perfect for spring.

1 cup (250ml)	soft butter	1 1/4 cups (300ml)	ground almonds
3/4 cup (175ml)	brown sugar	2/3 cup (150ml)	raspberry jam
2	eggs	5 oz (142g)	white chocolate
2 tsp (10ml)	vanilla	1/3 cup (75ml)	sour cream
2 1/4 cups (550ml)	all-purpose flour	1/4 cup (50ml)	whipping cream
1/4 tsp (1ml)	baking powder	40	raspberries
1/4 tsp (1ml)	baking soda		(optional)

Cream together butter and sugar until light and fluffy. Beat in eggs and vanilla.

In a separate bowl, mix together flour, baking powder, baking soda, and salt. Stir in ground almonds. Stir flour mixture into creamed mixture, in thirds. Cover and refrigerate for 1 hour.

Preheat oven to 350ºF (170ºC).

Between 2 sheets of waxed paper, roll out dough to 1/4-inch (5mm) thickness. Cut into 2 1/2-inch (6cm) hearts. (Scraps of dough can be rolled out again.) Place cookies 1 inch (2.5cm) apart on a parchment-lined cookie sheet.

Bake on the middle rack of the oven for 11 to 14 minutes or until edges are golden. Transfer to cooling racks.

When cookies are cool, spread 1/2 tsp (2ml) raspberry jam over the surface of each one. Melt white chocolate in a double boiler or stainless steel bowl over hot (not boiling) water. Stir in sour cream and whipping cream. Drizzle chocolate mixture over cookies. Set one raspberry (if using) into warm chocolate on each cookie.

Makes about 20 large cookies.

Easter Egg Cookies

Start a family tradition of baking and decorating Easter egg cookies. If you don't celebrate Easter, you can use this recipe to make edible Fabergé eggs.

1 cup (250ml)	soft butter
1 cup (250ml)	sugar
1	egg
1 tbsp (15ml)	cream
2 tsp (10ml)	vanilla
1/4 tsp (1ml)	lemon extract
3 1/4 cups (800ml)	all-purpose flour
1 tsp (5ml)	baking powder
1/4 tsp (1ml)	baking soda
1/2 tsp (2ml)	salt
1 1/2 cups (375ml)	Decorators' Icing (p. 121)

Cream together butter and sugar until light and fluffy. Beat in egg, then cream, vanilla, and lemon extract. In a separate bowl, combine flour with baking powder, baking soda, and salt. Stir flour mixture into creamed mixture in thirds.

Roll out dough between 2 sheets of waxed paper to 1/4-inch (5mm) thickness. Refrigerate for 1 hour.

Preheat oven to 375ºF (190ºC).

Cut out cookies with an egg-shaped cookie cutter. Place 2 inches (5cm) apart on a greased cookie sheet.

Bake on the middle rack of the oven for 12 to 14 minutes or until edges are darkened. Cool on cookie sheet for 2 minutes, then transfer to racks.

Make up several colours of decorator's icing and use to decorate cookies.

Makes about 2 dozen medium-sized cookies.

Maple Leaf Cookies

You will need a maple-leaf cookie cutter for these patriotic treats. I purchased mine in a bulk food store, but baker's supply stores and kitchen stores are another option.

1/2 cup (125ml)	soft butter
1/4 cup (50ml)	granulated sugar
1/4 cup (50ml)	tightly packed brown sugar
3 tbsp (50ml)	maple syrup
2 tsp (10ml)	vanilla
1	egg
1 1/2 cups (375ml)	all-purpose flour
1/4 tsp (1ml)	salt
2 oz (50g)	semi-sweet chocolate

Cream together butter and sugars until light and fluffy. Beat in syrup, vanilla, and egg. In a separate bowl, combine flour, and salt. Stir flour mixture into creamed mixture in thirds.

Melt chocolate in a double boiler or stainless steel bowl over hot (not boiling) water. Divide dough in half and stir chocolate into one half. Cover and refrigerate both halves for 1 hour.

Preheat oven to 375ºF (190ºC).

On a well-floured surface, roll out both portions of dough to 1/8-inch (3mm) thickness. Cut out 3-inch (8cm) rounds, then use a 2-inch (5cm) maple-leaf cutter to cut a leaf out of each round. Place a leaf of contrasting colour in the vacant centre of each round. (If dough becomes too soft and difficult to work with, return to the refrigerator to firm up.)

Bake on the middle rack of the oven for 7 minutes or until edges are darkened. Cool on cookie sheet for 2 minutes, then transfer to racks.

Makes about 2 dozen cookies.

Ice Cream Sandwiches

Shall I compare thee to a summer's day?
Thou art more yummy and cooler to the lips.

3 tbsp (50ml)	soft butter
1/2 cup (125ml)	sugar
1	egg
1 cup (250ml)	all-purpose flour
1/4 cup (50ml)	cocoa
1 tbsp (15ml)	chopped fresh mint
1 tsp (5ml)	ground ginger
1/2 tsp (2ml)	baking powder
1/4 tsp (1ml)	salt
3/4 cup (175ml)	vanilla ice cream

Preheat oven to 375ºF (190ºC).

Cream together butter and sugar until light and fluffy. Beat in egg. In a separate bowl, combine flour, cocoa, mint, ginger, baking powder, and salt. Stir flour mixture into creamed mixture in thirds.

Roll dough into 3/4-inch (2cm) balls and place on a parchment-lined baking sheet. Flatten slightly with a fork.

Bake on the middle rack of the oven for 7 to 10 minutes, or until set. Transfer to cooling racks.

When ready to serve, sandwich 1/2 tbsp (8ml) ice cream between two cookies.

Makes one dozen sandwiches.

Apple-Pie Cookies

Apple butter, homemade on small Mennonite farms, is just one of the wonderful products sold at the St. Jacob's Farmers' Market in Waterloo, Ontario. Beyond a doubt, local farmers' markets are the best place to purchase fresh organic produce, drug-free meats, and all the best foods.

1 cup (250ml)	soft butter	2 1/4 cup (550ml)	all-purpose flour
1/2 cup (125ml)	granulated sugar	1 tsp (5ml)	cinnamon
1/4 cup (50ml)	packed golden sugar	1/2 tsp (2ml)	ground cloves
1	egg	1/4 tsp (1ml)	freshly grated nutmeg
1/4 cup (50ml)	apple butter	1/4 tsp (1ml)	salt
1 tsp (5ml)	vanilla	1/2 cup (125ml)	apple pie filling

Cream together butter and sugars. Beat in egg, then apple butter and vanilla.

In a separate bowl, combine flour with cinnamon, cloves, nutmeg, and salt. Stir dry ingredients into butter mixture in thirds. Refrigerate for 1 hour.

Preheat oven to 350°F (170°C).

On a lightly-floured surface, roll out dough to 1/4-inch (3mm) thickness.

Use a 2-inch (5mm) cookie cutter to cut out rounds, then use a 1-inch (2.5cm) cutter to cut the centres out of half the rounds. (Centres can be re-rolled.) Place cookies 2 inches (5cm) apart on a parchment-lined cookie sheet.

Bake on the middle rack of the oven for 15 to 18 minutes or until golden. Transfer to cooling racks.

In a food processor, pulse the apple pie filling until there are no pieces larger than 1/4 inch (5mm). Spread apple filling on the whole cookie rounds and cover with the rings.

Makes about 14 cookies.

Pumpkin-Pie Squares

This cookie was inspired by the amazing pumpkin pies my chef husband makes for Thanksgiving dessert. The squares are equally delicious, and now we make both.

CRUST
1 1/2 cups (375ml)	flour
1/4 tsp (1ml)	salt
1/3 cup (75ml)	cold butter
1/4 cup (50ml)	sugar
1/4 cup (50ml)	cold water

FILLING
1 cup (250ml)	pumpkin pie filling
1/2 lb (250g)	cream cheese
1/2 cup (125ml)	brown sugar
1 tsp (5ml)	cinnamon
1/4 tsp (1ml)	freshly grated nutmeg

Preheat oven to 375°F (190°C).

Combine flour and salt, and rub in butter until the texture resembles coarse meal. Stir in sugar. Add water and mix by hand until a ball forms.

Press dough into an 8-inch (2L) square pan.

Beat together pumpkin pie filling, cream cheese, sugar, cinnamon, and nutmeg until creamy. Spread over pastry.

Bake for 40 minutes or until set. Let cool, then cut into 2-inch (5cm) squares.

Makes 16 squares.

Cranberry Logs

The scarlet colour of cranberries looks fantastic in these festive logs.
Make sure the purée is the consistency of thick jam.

1/2 cup (125ml)	dried cranberries		1 tsp (5ml)	vanilla
1/4 cup (50ml)	sugar		1 tbsp (15ml)	finely grated lemon zest
1/2 cup (125ml)	apple juice		1 1/4 cups (300ml)	all-purpose flour
1/2 cup (125ml)	soft butter		1/2 tsp (2ml)	baking powder
1/4 cup (50ml)	granulated sugar		1 cup (250ml)	powdered sugar
1/4 cup (50ml)	packed brown sugar		1 tbsp (15ml)	lemon juice
1	small egg			

Preheat oven to 350ºF (180ºC).

In a medium saucepan, combine cranberries, sugar and apple juice. Simmer for 15 minutes or until half of the juice is absorbed. Purée until smooth. (If the purée seems too thin, return to the pan and simmer until more liquid is reduced.)

Cream together butter and sugars until light and fluffy. Beat in egg and vanilla, then stir in lemon zest. In a separate bowl, combine flour and baking powder. Stir flour mixture into creamed mixture in thirds.

Divide dough into four pieces and press each piece into a 2x4-inch (5x10cm) rectangle, 3/4 inch (2cm) thick. Using your fingers, make a 2 1/2x1 inch (6x2.5cm) trough along the centre of each rectangle. Fill the trough with cranberry filling.

Bake on ungreased baking sheet for 15 to 18 minutes or until golden. Transfer to cooling racks.

Whisk together sugar and lemon juice until smooth, and drizzle over the surface of the cranberry logs. Cut logs crosswise into 1-inch (2.5cm) strips.

Makes about 16 cookies.

Maple Pumpkin Cookies

*Maple syrup and pumpkin — a delicious duo — are combined
in these cookies. They're ideal for sharing with a friend while you wait for
Linus' Great Pumpkin to rise out of your Hallowe'en patch.*

1/2 cup (125ml)	soft butter
1/2 cup (125ml)	packed brown sugar
1/2 cup (125ml)	granulated sugar
1	egg
3 tbsp (50ml)	maple syrup
1/2 cup (125ml)	canned pumpkin
2 cups (500ml)	all-purpose flour
1 tsp (5ml)	baking soda
1 tsp (5ml)	cinnamon
1/4 tsp (1ml)	freshly ground nutmeg
1/2 tsp (2ml)	salt

Preheat oven to 350°F (180°C).

Cream butter and sugars until light and fluffy. Beat in egg, maple syrup, and pumpkin.

Mix together flour, baking soda, cinnamon, nutmeg, and salt. Stir flour mixture into creamed butter in thirds.

Drop heaping tablespoons of dough on a greased cookie sheet.

Bake on middle rack of the oven for 10 to 12 minutes or until edges are browned. Transfer to racks to cool.

Makes about 3 dozen cookies.

Pumpkin-Seed Cookies

*I have been collecting cookie cutters for years, so at Hallowe'en we
pull can out a great assortment of cats, pumpkins, and witches on broomsticks.
If your local market does not carry pumpkin seeds, look in a health-food store or
a specialty market. Mexican markets carry them under the name "pepitas."*

3/4 cup (175ml)	unsalted pumpkin seeds
4 oz (125g)	chocolate chips
1 cup (250ml)	soft butter
1 cup (250ml)	sugar
2 1/4 cups (550ml)	all-purpose flour
1 tsp (5ml)	cinnamon
1/4 tsp (1ml)	salt
1	egg
1 tsp (5ml)	milk
2 tbsp (25ml)	orange sugar

Preheat oven to 325°F (160°C).

In a food processor, pulse pumpkin seeds until fine. Mix together flour, cinnamon, salt and pumpkin seeds.

Melt chocolate in a stainless steel bowl or double boiler over hot (not boiling) water. Cream butter and sugar until light and fluffy, then stir in chocolate. Stir dry ingredients into chocolate mixture in thirds.

On a lightly-floured surface, roll out dough to 1/4-inch (5mm) thickness. Cut with 2 inch (5cm) Hallowe'en cookie cutters and place 1 inch (2.5cm) apart on a parchment-lined cookie sheet. Stir together egg and milk and brush on tops of cookies. Sprinkle with orange sugar.

Bake on middle rack of the oven for 17 to 20 minutes or until firm. Transfer to cooling rack.

Makes about 3 dozen cookies.

Mascarpone-Filled Snaps

This elegant cookie is a perfect indulgence for the year's grand finale.

1/2 cup (125ml)	soft butter
2/3 cup (175ml)	golden syrup
1/4 cup (50ml)	packed golden sugar
1 tsp (5ml)	ground ginger
1 cup (250ml)	all-purpose flour
1 tbsp (15ml)	brandy

FILLING

1/2 cup (125ml)	mascarpone cheese
1 tbsp (15ml)	strong brewed espresso
1 tbsp (15ml)	sugar
1/2 cup (125ml)	whipping cream

Preheat the oven to 350ºF (180ºC).

Combine butter, syrup, sugar, and ginger in a heavy-bottomed saucepan over medium-high heat. Simmer for 2 minutes, stirring frequently. Remove from heat and whisk in flour and brandy.

Drop tablespoons of dough 4 inches (10cm) apart on a greased cookie sheet.

Bake on the middle rack of the oven for 8 to 10 minutes or until golden.

Cool slightly, then roll each cookie around a handle that is 1 inch (2.5cm) in diameter. (If the cookies loose their flexibility, return them to the oven to soften.)

Beat together mascarpone, espresso, and sugar. Whip cream until firm and fold into mascarpone mixture. Pipe or spoon filling into the snaps.

Makes about 12 snaps.

All Sorts of Cookies

This chapter is a mixed bag of delights. These recipes were developed in our test kitchen, often with the help of friends, neighbours, and of course, children. Inventing cookies is great fun!

First we brought together all the yummy ingredients we could find and chose our favourite combinations. Coffee and chocolate, toffee and chocolate, nuts and chocolate, chocolate and chocolate, all came together in great cookie ideas.

Next we decided on the shape of the cookie — a drop cookie, a rolled cookie, or something altogether new. Happy Faces came to life when my adorable three-year-old came into the kitchen with a new, yellow, happy-face toy, pretending it was a cookie. Out of the mouths of babes!

The next step was to lay out a baking plan. We found the information to gauge the ratio of ingredients needed for a successful cookie experiment. in "The Science behind the Cookie" (see p. xiv).

The final step was the baking. Often it took two or three bakings before a recipe was perfected. We can only hope that you have half as much fun making and eating these cookies as we had inventing them!

Happy Faces

For kids only! This is a fun recipe to try with younger helpers.
Try to achieve a bright yellow colour for the icing.

1 cup (250ml)	soft butter
1 cup (250ml)	sugar
2	eggs
1 tsp (5ml)	vanilla
1 1/2 cups (375ml)	sifted all-purpose flour
1/2 tsp (2ml)	baking powder
1/4 tsp (1ml)	salt
3/4 cup (175ml)	yellow Decorators' Icing (p. 121)
1/4 lb (125g)	black licorice strings

Cream together butter and sugar until light and fluffy. Beat in eggs, one at a time, then vanilla.

Mix together flour, baking powder and salt. Stir flour mixture into creamed butter in thirds. Roll out between two sheets of waxed paper to 1/4-inch (5mm) thickness. Refrigerate for 1 hour.

Preheat oven to 350ºF (180ºC).

Cut out circles using a 3-inch (8cm) round cookie cutter. Place 2 inches (5cm) apart on a parchment-lined cookie sheet.

Bake on the middle rack of the oven for 7 to 10 minutes or until edges are darkened. Transfer to cooling racks.

Spread yellow icing over cookies to cover. Cut licorice into short pieces for eyes and longer pieces for smile, and arrange on icing before it sets. Let cookies set for 1 hour.

Makes about 18 cookies.

Treasure Chests

Even the youngest children can help with this recipe. Buy the brightest candied fruit you can find to represent the jewels in the chest — cherries make nice rubies.

1 cup (250ml)	soft butter
1/4 cup (50ml)	firmly packed brown sugar
1/4 cup (50ml)	granulated sugar
1	egg
1 tbsp (15ml)	lemon juice
1 1/2 cups (375ml)	sifted all-purpose flour
1/2 cup (125ml)	rice flour
1/2 cup (125ml)	candied fruit

Cream together butter and sugars. Beat in egg and lemon juice. Combine the all-purpose flour and the rice flour and stir into the creamed mixture until smooth. Refrigerate for 30 minutes.

Preheat oven to 375°F (190°C).

On a lightly-floured surface, roll out dough to 1/2-inch (1cm) thickness. Cut dough into rectangles 1 1/2x2-inch (4x5cm) rectangles. Press candied fruit into cookies to resemble treasure chests.

Bake for 10 to 12 minutes or until edges are golden.

Makes about 2 dozen cookies.

Pecan Bliss Cookies

These delicious cookies look best if they are well-coated in powdered sugar.
Give them a second dusting just before serving.

1/2 cup (125ml)	pecan pieces
1 cup (250ml)	powdered sugar
1 cup (250ml)	soft butter
1 tsp (5ml)	vanilla
1 3/4 cups (425ml)	all-purpose flour
2 tbsp (25ml)	cocoa
1 tsp (5ml)	cinnamon
1 1/2 cups (375ml)	powdered sugar (for garnish)

Preheat oven to 350ºF (180ºC).

Spread pecans on a cookie sheet and bake for 10 minutes or until golden. Let cool, then process with sugar in a food processor until fine. Add butter, then vanilla, and pulse until mixture is smooth. Transfer mixture to a medium bowl.

In a separate bowl, combine flour, cocoa, and cinnamon. Stir into creamed mixture in thirds. Roll dough into 1-inch (2.5cm) balls and place 2 inches (5cm) apart on a parchment-lined cookie sheet.

Bake on the middle rack of the oven for 13 to 15 minutes or until firm. Roll in powdered sugar while warm, then transfer to cooling racks.

Makes about 30 cookies.

Chocolate Pistachio Log

This is a favourite treat for a hot summer day when turning on the oven is unthinkable.

7 oz (200g)	semi-sweet chocolate
3 tbsp (50ml)	butter
1/3 cup (75ml)	sugar
1 cup (250ml)	pistachios, chopped
1/4 cup (50ml)	chocolate cookie crumbs
1/4 cup (50ml)	candied orange
2	egg yolks

In a double boiler or stainless steel bowl over hot (not boiling) water, melt the chocolate with the butter. Stir in the sugar, pistachios, cookie crumbs, and orange. Remove from heat and stir in the yolks, one at a time.

Form into a 1 1/2-inch (4cm) log. Wrap in waxed paper or plastic wrap and refrigerate overnight.

To serve, cut chilled log into 1/2-inch (1cm) slices.

Makes about 2 dozen cookies.

Gooey Toffee Cookies

Nothing beats a big chocolate cookie with a gooey toffee centre. I suggested putting these cookies on the cover of the book because I love their old-fashioned look.

1/2 cup (125ml)	all-purpose flour
1 tsp (5ml)	baking powder
1/4 tsp (1ml)	salt
1 lb (125g)	semi-sweet chocolate, chopped
1/4 cup (125ml)	soft butter
1 cup (250ml)	packed brown sugar
3/4 cup (175ml)	granulated sugar
4	eggs
2 tbsp (25ml)	coffee liqueur
1 tbsp (15ml)	vanilla
5 oz (140g)	toffee

Melt chocolate in a stainless steel bowl over hot (not boiling) water.

Sift together flour, baking powder and salt. Cream together butter and sugars. Beat in eggs, one at a time, then liqueur, vanilla, and chocolate.

Stir flour mixture into creamed mixture in thirds. Chop toffee and fold into dough. Refrigerate for 1 hour.

Preheat oven to 325ºF (160ºC).

Drop tablespoons of dough on parchment-lined cookie sheets

Bake on the middle rack of the oven for 10 to 12 minutes or until set but still gooey.

Makes about 2 dozen cookies.

Peanut Pecan Cookies

The combination of peanuts and pecans give this cookie a double crunch.

1 1/2 cups (375ml)	all-purpose flour
1/2 tsp (2ml)	baking powder
1/3 cup (75ml)	soft butter
1/2 cup (125ml)	packed brown sugar
1/2 cup (125ml)	granulated sugar
1/2 cup (125ml)	peanut butter
1	egg
1 tsp (5ml)	vanilla
1 cup (250ml)	pecan pieces

Preheat oven to 350ºF (170ºC).

Sift together flour and baking powder. In a separate bowl, cream together butter and sugars until light and fluffy. Beat in peanut butter, egg and vanilla.

Stir dry ingredients into creamed mixture in thirds. Fold in pecan pieces.

Roll dough into 2-inch (5cm) balls and place 2 inches (5cm) apart on parchment-lined cookie sheets. Flatten cookies with a damp fork.

Bake on the middle rack of the oven for 15 to 18 minutes or until golden brown at the edges. Let cool on racks.

Makes about 12 large cookies.

Ginger Marmalade Rings

This pretty cookie is a personal favourite. Ginger marmalade is a versatile ingredient I always keep on hand, not only for cookies but also to serve with fresh scones or to use as a glaze for chicken or fish.

1 cup (250ml)	soft butter
3/4 cup (175ml)	brown sugar
2	eggs
2 tsp (10ml)	vanilla
2 1/4 cups (550ml)	all-purpose flour
1/4 tsp (1ml)	baking powder
1/4 tsp (1ml)	baking soda
1/4 tsp (1ml)	salt
1 1/4 cups (300ml)	ground almonds
1/2 cup (125ml)	ginger marmalade

Cream together butter and sugar until light and fluffy. Beat in eggs and vanilla.

Mix together flour, baking powder, baking soda, and salt. Stir in ground almonds. Stir dry ingredients into creamed mixture in thirds. Cover and refrigerate for 1 hour.

Preheat oven to 325°F (160°C).

Between two sheets of waxed paper, roll out dough to 1/4-inch (5mm) thickness. Cut into 2-inch (5cm) rounds. (Pieces of dough can be rolled out again.) Cut a 1/2-inch (5mm) hole in the centre of half the rounds to make rings. (The centre hole can be heart shaped.) Place 1 inch (2.5cm) apart on a parchment-lined cookie sheet.

Bake on the middle rack of the oven for 20 minutes or until golden. Transfer to cooling racks.

When cool, spread 1/4 tsp (1ml) marmalade over each whole round, top with a ring, and press gently to secure. If desired, place a little additional marmalade in the open centre of the cookies.

Makes about 20 cookies.

Rum Pots

Yo-ho-ho and a bottle of rum — Cookies fit for a pirate!

1 cup (250ml)	soft butter
3/4 cup (175ml)	brown sugar
1	egg
2 tsp (10ml)	vanilla
2 cups (500ml)	all-purpose flour
2 tsp (10ml)	ground ginger
1/4 tsp (1ml)	baking powder
1/4 tsp (1ml)	salt

FILLING

1/3 cup (75ml)	butter
3/4 cup (175ml)	icing sugar
1 tbsp (15ml)	dark rum

Preheat oven to 350ºF (180ºC).

Cream together butter and sugar until light and fluffy. Beat in eggs and vanilla.

Mix together flour, ginger, baking powder and salt. Stir dry ingredients into creamed butter in thirds. Drop teaspoons of dough 2 inches (5cm) apart on a parchment-lined cookie sheet.

Bake on the middle rack of the oven for 12 to 15 minutes or until golden. Transfer to cooling racks.

Cream together butter, icing sugar, and rum. Spread 1 tsp (5ml) of filling on the bottom of a cookie and use a second cookie to make a sandwich.

Makes about 2 dozen cookies.

Persimmon Cookies

Look for persimmons on grocery shelves during the winter months. The fruit should be smooth textured, bright red-orange, and completely ripened.

1/2 cup (125ml)	soft butter
1 cup (250ml)	sugar
1	egg
1 cup (250ml)	mashed persimmon
2 cups (500ml)	flour
1 tsp (5ml)	baking powder
1 tsp (5ml)	cinnamon
1/2 tsp (2ml)	freshly grated nutmeg
1/4 tsp (1ml)	salt
1 cup (250ml)	golden raisins
1 cup (250ml)	chopped walnuts

Preheat oven to 350ºF (180ºC).

Cream together butter and sugar until light and fluffy. Beat in egg, then persimmon. In a separate bowl, mix flour, baking powder, cinnamon, nutmeg, and salt.

Stir flour mixture into creamed butter in thirds. Fold in raisins and walnuts. Drop heaping teaspoons of dough on a parchment-lined cookie sheet.

Bake on the middle rack of the oven for 12 to 15 minutes or until edges are golden. Transfer to cooling racks.

Makes about 2 dozen cookies.

Honey-Roasted Cashew Cookies

These cashews are honey-coated before being roasted, and the result is pure heaven. Bake them into these cookies for a special treat. If you can't find them, substitute pralines.

1/2 cup (125ml)	soft butter
3/4 cup (175ml)	granulated sugar
3/4 cup (175ml)	brown sugar
1 cup (250ml)	cashew butter OR peanut butter
2	eggs
1 tsp (5ml)	vanilla
1 1/2 cup (375ml)	all-purpose flour
1 tsp (5ml)	baking powder
1 1/2 cups (375ml)	chopped honey-roasted cashews

Preheat oven to 350ºF (180ºC).

Cream together butter and sugar until light and fluffy. Beat in sugars and cashew butter. Beat in eggs, one at a time, then vanilla.

Mix together flour and baking soda. Stir flour mixture into cashew butter mixture in thirds. Fold in cashews.

Drop heaping half-tablespoons of dough 2 inches (4cm) apart on an ungreased cookie sheet.

Bake on middle rack of the oven for 8 to 10 minutes or until golden. Transfer to cooling racks.

Makes about 4 dozen cookies.

Chocolate Hazelnut Cookies

*Chocolate hazelnut spread is great in cookies, but it also makes
a lovely instant glaze or coating for cookies and cakes.*

1 cup (250ml)	soft butter
1 cup (250ml)	packed brown sugar
1/2 cup (125ml)	chocolate hazelnut spread
1	egg
1 cup (250ml)	all-purpose flour
1 tsp (5ml)	baking soda
1/2 tsp (2ml)	baking powder
1/4 tsp (1ml)	salt
1 cup (250ml)	crushed corn flakes
36 (about 1 cup/250ml)	hazelnuts

Cream together butter and sugar until light and fluffy. Beat in chocolate hazelnut spread and egg.

Mix together flour, baking soda, baking powder, and salt. Add corn flakes. Stir flour mixture into hazelnut mixture in thirds. Refrigerate for 1 hour.

Preheat oven to 375ºF (190ºC).

Roll dough into 1-inch (2.5cm) balls and place 2 inches (5cm) apart on a parchment-lined cookie sheet. Flatten with a fork and press a hazelnut into the centre of each cookie.

Bake on the middle rack of the oven for 10 to 13 minutes or until golden. Transfer to a cooling rack.

Makes about 4 dozen cookies.

Pecan Caramel Clusters

A more decadent cookie would be difficult to find. Biting into the pecan caramel centre of this delectable creation is an exercise in indulgence.

1 cup (250ml)	butter
1 cup (250ml)	sugar
1	egg
1 tsp (5ml)	vanilla
2 oz (50g)	semi-sweet chocolate
2 1/2 cups (625ml)	all-purpose flour
1 tsp (5ml)	baking powder
1/4 tsp (1ml)	salt
36	pecan caramel clusters

Melt chocolate in a double boiler or stainless steel bowl over hot (not boiling) water. Let cool slightly.

Cream together butter and sugar until light and fluffy. Beat in egg and vanilla. Stir chocolate into creamed butter.

In a separate bowl, mix together flour, baking powder and salt. Stir flour mixture into chocolate mixture in thirds. Refrigerate for 1 hour.

Preheat oven to 350ºF (180ºC). Roll dough into 1-inch (2.5cm) balls and place 3 inches (8cm) apart on a parchment-lined cookie sheet. Press a caramel cluster into the centre of each cookie.

Bake on the middle rack of the oven for 10 to 13 minutes or until firm. Cool on cookie sheet for 1 minute, then transfer to racks.

Makes about 2 dozen cookies.

Red-Pepper Jellies

The red-pepper centre is the jewel in this cookie's crown.

1 1/4 cup (300ml)	soft butter
1 cup (250ml)	sugar
1	egg
1 tsp (5ml)	vanilla
2 cups (500ml)	all-purpose flour
1/2 tsp (2ml)	baking powder
1/2 tsp (2ml)	cinnamon
1/3 cup (75ml)	red pepper jelly

Cream together butter and sugar until light and fluffy. Beat in egg, then vanilla.

In a separate bowl, mix together flour, baking powder, and cinnamon. Stir flour mixture into creamed butter in thirds. Wrap dough in plastic and refrigerate for 30 minutes.

Preheat oven to 350ºF (180ºC).

Roll dough into 1 1/4-inch (3cm) balls and place 1 inch (2.5cm) apart on a greased cookie sheet. Make an indentation in each ball with your thumb, and fill with 1/2 tsp (2ml) red pepper jelly.

Bake on the middle rack of the oven for 12 to 15 minutes or until edges are golden. Transfer to cooling racks.

Makes about 2 dozen cookies.

Fuzzy Peaches

*Cookies and candies — a perfect team —
are ideally suited to this kid-friendly treat.*

1 cup (250ml)	soft butter
1 cup (250ml)	packed brown sugar
1	egg
1 tsp (5ml)	vanilla
2 tbsp (25ml)	peach jam
3 cups (750ml)	all-purpose flour
1/2 tsp (2ml)	baking soda
1/4 tsp (1ml)	salt
3 tbsp (50ml)	orange decorators' sugar
1 cup (250ml)	Fuzzy Peach candy

Cream together butter and sugar until light and fluffy. Beat in egg, vanilla and jam. In a separate bowl, combine flour, baking soda, and salt. Stir flour mixture into butter mixture in thirds.

Knead for 2 to 3 minutes or until dough is pliable. Roll dough into a 1 1/2-inch (4cm) log and wrap in plastic or parchment. Refrigerate for 2 hours.

Preheat oven to 375ºF (190ºC).

Roll dough log in orange sugar. Cut log into 1/2-inch (1cm) slices and press a Fuzzy Peach into each cookie. Place 2 inches (5cm) apart on a parchment-lined cookie sheet.

Bake on the middle rack of the oven for 7 minutes or until golden. Transfer to cooling racks.

Makes about 3 dozen cookies.

Cinnamon Poppy Seed Pinwheels

Pinwheels are terrific for adding dimension to a tray of cookies. This recipe is a reworking of an old classic, with almond paste added to the traditional cinnamon.

1 cup (250ml)	soft butter
1/4 cup (50ml)	packed golden sugar
1	egg
1 tsp (5ml)	vanilla
1 1/4 cups (300ml)	all-purpose flour
1 tbsp (15ml)	cinnamon
1/2 tsp (2ml)	baking powder
1/4 tsp (1ml)	salt
1/2 cup (125ml)	almond paste
1/4 cup (50ml)	poppy seeds

Cream together butter and sugar until light and fluffy. Beat in egg and vanilla.

In a separate bowl, combine flour, cinnamon, baking powder, and salt. Stir flour mixture into creamed butter in thirds. Roll between two pieces of plastic into a square, 1/4-inch (5mm) thick. Refrigerate for 1 hour.

Preheat oven to 375ºF (190ºC).

Stir together almond paste and poppy seeds. Roll out paste and press into the top of the dough and roll up, like a jelly roll. Place in freezer for 10 minutes. Cut roll into 1/2-inch (1cm) slices and place on a parchment-lined cookie sheet.

Bake on the middle rack of the oven for 10 minutes or until edges are golden. Transfer to cooling rack.

Makes about 2 dozen cookies.

Butter-Pecan Morsels

Creaming the butter and sugar together incorporates air into the mixture at an early stage. The result is a light, tender cookie.

2 cups (500ml)	soft butter
1/2 cup (125ml)	granulated sugar
1/4 cup (50ml)	packed brown sugar
1	egg
1 tbsp (15ml)	vanilla
3 1/2 cups (875ml)	all-purpose flour
1 tsp (5ml)	baking powder
1 1/2 cups (375ml)	chopped pecans

Preheat oven to 350ºF (180ºC).

Cream together butter and sugars until light and fluffy. Beat in egg and vanilla.

In a separate bowl, combine flour and baking powder. Stir flour mixture into creamed butter in thirds. Fold in pecans.

Drop rounded teaspoons of dough on a parchment-lined cookie sheet.

Bake for 10 minutes or until golden. Transfer to cooling racks.

Makes about 3 dozen cookies.

Fairy Cookies

I love to hunt for old cookie cutters at antique stores and flea markets. Baking this cookie gives me the chance to use some of the more fanciful cutters in my collection.

1/2 cup (125ml)	soft butter
1/2 cup (125ml)	sugar
2	egg whites
1 cup (250ml)	all-purpose flour
1/2 cup (125ml)	ground almonds
1/4 cup (50ml)	pink decorators' sugar

Cream together butter and sugar until light and fluffy. Beat in 1 egg white.

In a separate bowl, mix together flour and ground almonds. Stir flour mixture into creamed mixture in thirds. Refrigerate for 1 hour.

Preheat oven to 375°F (190°C).

Roll dough out on a lightly-floured surface to 1/4-inch (5mm) thickness. Use 1 1/2-inch (4cm) cookie cutters to cut out fanciful shapes. Place 2 inches (5cm) apart on a parchment-lined cookie sheet. Beat remaining egg white slightly. Brush cookies with beaten egg white and dust with decorators' sugar.

Bake on the middle rack of the oven for 8 to 10 minutes or until edges are golden. Transfer to cooling racks.

Makes about 2 dozen cookies.

Chocolate Hazelnut Pinwheels

Chocolate hazelnut spread is a marvelous convenience food. I keep it on hand to use as an instant frosting for cakes, cupcakes, and cookies.

1/2 cup (125ml)	soft butter
1/2 cup (125ml)	sugar
1	egg yolk
3 tbsp (50ml)	milk
1 tsp (5ml)	vanilla
1 1/2 cups (375ml)	flour
1 tsp (5ml)	baking powder
1/4 tsp (1ml)	salt
1/4 cup (50ml)	chocolate hazelnut spread

Cream together butter and sugar until light and fluffy. Beat in yolk, milk and vanilla. In a separate bowl, mix together flour, baking powder, and salt. Stir flour mixture in creamed butter in thirds. Divide dough in half, and stir chocolate hazelnut spread into one half of the dough.

Between 2 sheets of waxed paper, roll both portions of dough into rectangular sheets, 1/8 inch (3mm) thick. Place one sheet over the other and roll up into a log, as for a jelly roll. Wrap in plastic and place in freezer for 15 mintues.

Preheat oven to 375ºF (190ºC).

Cut log into 1/2-inch (1cm) slices and place 1 inch (2.5cm) apart on a greased cookie sheet.

Bake on the middle rack of the oven for 13 to 15 minutes or until edges are golden. Transfer to cooling racks.

Makes about 2 dozen cookies.

Strawberry Shortcake Cookies

*Strawberry shortcake cookies! Why not? We have transformed
this traditional desert into a cookie format. For extra authenticity,
add a thin layer of whipped cream on top of the jam.*

1/3 cup (75ml)	soft butter
1 cup (250ml)	sugar
2	eggs
1 tsp (5ml)	vanilla
2 cups (500ml)	flour
1/4 tsp (1ml)	salt
1/2 cup (125ml)	strawberry jam

Preheat oven to 375ºF (190ºC).

Cream together butter and sugar. Beat in eggs, one at a time, then vanilla. In a separate bowl mix together flour and salt. Stir flour mixture into creamed mixture in thirds.

Between 2 sheets of waxed paper, roll out dough to 1/4-inch (5mm) thickness. Place in freezer for 15 minutes. Cut dough into rounds using 2-inch (5cm) cookie cutters. Place 2 inches (5cm) apart on a parchment-lined cookie sheet.

Bake for 13 to 15 minutes or until golden. Transfer to cooling racks.

Once cool, spread strawberry jam on the top of half of the cookies and top with the plain cookies to make a sandwich. Add a drop of jam on top of each one.

Makes about 12 cookies.

Tropical Treats

*When my baby smiles at me, I go to Rio. And when
I don't have time to live out old song lyrics, I make these
cookies to bring a taste of the tropics into my kitchen.*

3/4 cup (175ml)	soft butter
1 cup (250ml)	packed brown sugar
2	eggs
2	very ripe bananas
1 1/2 cups (375ml)	all-purpose flour
1 tsp (5ml)	ground ginger
1 tsp (5ml)	baking powder
2 cups (500ml)	granola
1/2 cup (125ml)	chopped dried mango
1/2 cup (125ml)	chopped candied ginger

Preheat oven to 350°F (180°C).

Cream together butter and sugar until light and fluffy. Beat in eggs, one at a time, then banana. In a separate bowl, combine flour, ground ginger and baking powder, then add granola.

Stir flour mixture into creamed mixture in thirds. Fold in chopped mango and ginger. Drop heaping tablespoons of dough on a parchment-lined cookie sheets.

Bake on the middle rack of the oven for 15 to 18 minutes or until golden. Transfer to cooling racks.

Makes about 3 dozen cookies.

Granola Clusters

You just have to love cookies these no-bake cookies!

5 oz (142g)	milk chocolate
2 oz (50g)	semi-sweet chocolate
1 cup (250ml)	slivered almonds
1 cup (250ml)	granola

In a double boiler or stainless steel bowl over hot (not boiling) water, melt the chocolates together. Stir in the almonds and granola.

Drop heaping teaspoons of dough on a parchment-lined cookie sheet. Refrigerate, uncovered, for 2 hours or until firm. Store in the refrigerator.

Makes about 3 dozen clusters.

Chocolate Almond Biscuits

*It is essential all utensils used for beating egg whites be absolutely clean.
A trace of oil or protein on the beaters or the bowl may prevent
the whites from obtaining any volume. Rinse all utensils with vinegar
and then with water and allow to dry completely.*

1 cup (250ml)	ground almonds
2/3 cup (150ml)	sugar
1/4 tsp (1ml)	salt
1/2 cup (125ml)	milk
1/2 tsp (2ml)	vanilla
1/3 cup (75ml)	softened butter
3/4 cup (175ml)	sifted all-purpose flour
2	egg whites
Pinch	cream of tartar
6 oz (180g)	semi-sweet chocolate

Preheat oven to 350ºF (180ºC).

Whisk together almonds and half the sugar. Beat in salt, milk, vanilla, and butter. Stir in the flour in thirds. In a clean glass, stainless steel or copper-lined bowl, beat the egg whites with the cream of tartar until they begin to hold their shape. Increase the speed to medium high, and beat in the remaining sugar until stiff peaks form. Fold the egg whites into the dough.

Drop teaspoons of dough 2 inches (5cm) apart on a greased cookie sheet. Drop the sheet onto the counter to flatten out the cookies.

Bake on the middle rack of the oven for 10 minutes or until edges are golden. Cool on cookie sheet for 2 minutes, then transfer to racks.

In a double boiler or stainless steel bowl over hot (not boiling) water, melt the chocolate. Dip one side of the cookie into the chocolate to cover and return to racks to set.

Makes about 3 dozen cookies.

Chocolate-Dipped Hazelnut Fingers

These cookies are lovely but delicate.
Take care in the dipping because they break easily.

1/2 cup (125ml)	soft butter
2 tbsp (25ml)	packed golden sugar
1 tsp (5ml)	vanilla
1 cup (250ml)	ground hazelnuts
3/4 cup (175ml)	all-purpose flour
Pinch	salt
6 oz (170g)	semi-sweet chocolate

Preheat oven to 350ºF (180ºC).

Cream together butter and sugar until light and fluffy. Beat in vanilla. In a separate bowl, combine hazelnuts, flour and salt. Stir flour mixture into creamed mixture in thirds.

Shape the dough into 3x1-inch (8x2.5cm) fingers and place 2 inches (5cm) apart on a greased cookie sheet.

Bake on the middle rack of the oven for 15 minutes or until golden. Transfer to cooling racks.

In a double boiler or stainless steel bowl over hot (not boiling) water, melt the chocolate. Dip cooled cookies into the chocolate so that about a third of each finger is covered in chocolate.

Makes 2 dozen cookies.

Chocolate-Hazelnut Tarts

Yummy! These tarts are a sure hit with any crowd.

1/2 cup (125ml)	cold, cubed butter
1 cup (250ml)	all-purpose flour
1/4 tsp (1ml)	salt
2 oz (50g)	cream cheese
1/2 cup (125ml)	chocolate hazelnut spread
2 tbsp (25ml)	golden syrup
1	egg
3/4 cup (175ml)	whole hazelnuts

Preheat oven to 350ºF (180ºC).

Combine flour and salt, and rub in butter until the texture is coarse and mealy. Cut in cream cheese. Press 1 1/2 tbsp (20ml) dough into each cup of a mini-muffin or tart tin.

Combine hazelnut spread, syrup, egg, and nuts. Spoon into pastry shells.

Bake on the middle rack of the oven for 20 minutes or until set.

Makes about 2 dozen tarts.

Spelt Raisin Cookies

Spelt flour is an excellent alternative to wheat flour for those who cannot tolerate wheat. Unlike rice or bean flours, spelt flour has a high gluten content, which enables it to rise and gives goods baked with it a more pleasing texture.

1 cup (250ml)	granulated sugar
1 cup (250ml)	brown sugar
1 cup (250ml)	soft butter
2	eggs
1/4 cup (50ml)	35% cream
1 tsp (5ml)	vanilla
2 cups (500ml)	spelt flour
1 tsp (5ml)	cinnamon
1 tsp (5ml)	baking powder
1/2 tsp (2ml)	baking soda
1/2 tsp (2ml)	salt
2 1/4 cups (550ml)	quick-cooking oats
1 cup (250ml)	plumped raisins

Preheat oven to 350ºF (180ºC).

Cream together sugars and butter. Beat in eggs, cream, and vanilla.

In a separate bowl, sift together flour, cinnamon, baking powder, baking soda, and salt. Stir oats into dry ingredients along with raisins. Fold dry ingredients into creamed mixture.

Roll dough into 1-inch (2.5cm) balls and place 1 inch (2.5cm) apart on an ungreased cookie sheet. Do not flatten.

Bake for 13 to 16 minutes or until edges are darkened.

Makes about 4 dozen

Blueberry Napoleons

*Where would I be without frozen puff pastry? It is one of the best
high-quality convenience foods available. I use it to prepare everything
from hors d'oeuvres to desserts in record time with minimal fuss.*

8 oz m (250g)	frozen puff pastry, thawed
1/2 cup (125ml)	blueberry jam
1/2 cup (125ml)	whipping cream
2 tbsp (25ml)	powdered sugar

Preheat oven to 400ºF (200ºC).

On a floured surface, roll out pastry to 12-inch square. Cut into 2-inch (5cm) squares and place
1 inch (2.5cm) apart on a parchment-lined cookie sheet.

Bake on the middle rack of the oven for 10 to 12 minutes or until golden. Transfer to cooling racks.

Whip cream until stiff. Spread blueberry jam over surface of half of the cooled squares. Cover
with whipped cream, top with the plain squares, and dust with powdered sugar.

Makes 18 napoleons.

Chocolate Cinnamon Twists

Here is another chance to use frozen puff pastry to prepare something delicious in short order. These twists are so elegant, people will think you've been training as a pastry chef on the sly.

8 oz (250g)	frozen puff pastry, thawed
1/4 cup (50ml)	melted butter
2 tbsp (25ml)	cinnamon
2 tbsp (25ml)	sugar
5 oz (142g)	semi-sweet chocolate

Preheat oven to 400ºF (200ºC).

On a lightly-floured surface, roll out pastry to 1/8-inch (3mm) thickness. Brush surface with melted butter, and dust with cinnamon and sugar.

Cut pastry into strips 1/2-inch (1cm) wide and the length of the pastry. Twist each strip to make a long twisted rope. Place twists 1 inch (2.5cm) apart on a parchment-lined cookie sheet.

Bake on the middle rack of the oven for 12 to 15 minutes or until golden. Transfer to cooling racks.

In a double boiler or stainless steel bowl over hot (not boiling) water, melt the chocolate. Dip one end of the twists in the chocolate to coat and return to cooling racks to let the chocolate set.

Makes about 2 dozen twists.

Low-Fat Cookies

In "The Science Behind the Cookie," I described a cookie as containing about 20 to 25 percent fat. It would seem then, that the term low-fat cookie is an oxymoron, and in many ways it is. Before setting out to make low-fat cookies, you need to change your expectations. Low-fat cookies won't have the richness or texture of traditional cookies but they can still be a good treat. When setting out to make a low-fat treat, it is best to decide not to imitate full-fat favourites. If you love double chocolate chunk cookies, you won't be happy with an insipid imitation — make Date Walnut Bonbons instead. They are so sweet and rich that you won't feel like you're missing a thing.

Lemon Meringue Squares

These squares are like lemon meringue pie, but with half the calories.

1 cup (250ml)	all-purpose flour
Pinch	salt
1/4 cup (50ml)	powdered sugar
1/4 cup (50 ml)	cold butter, cubed
1	egg white, lightly beaten
1 tbsp (15ml)	skim milk

LEMON FILLING

1/3 cup (75ml)	sugar
1 tbsp (15ml)	cornstarch
Pinch	salt
1 tbsp (15ml)	lemon zest, finely grated
1/4 cup (50ml)	water
2 tbsp (25ml)	lemon juice
1	egg, beaten

MERINGUE

2	egg whites
1/4 cup (50ml)	sugar
Pinch	cream of tartar

Preheat oven to 350ºF (180ºC).

Combine flour and salt. Rub in butter until the mixture resembles coarse crumbs. Stir in sugar, egg white, and milk. Press dough into a lightly-greased 8-inch (2L) square pan.

Bake on the middle rack of the oven for 15 minutes or until set. Remove pan from oven and increase oven heat to 400ºF (200ºC).

Meanwhile, make lemon filling. In a small nonreactive pan, stir together sugar, cornstarch, salt, and lemon zest. Over medium heat, whisk in water, lemon juice, and egg. Whisk constantly until mixture thickens. Spread oven baked pastry.

In a clean stainless steel, glass or copper-lined bowl beat egg whites with cream of tartar on low speed until firm but not stiff. Increase speed to medium high, beat in sugar, and continue to beat until stiff. Spoon meringue over lemon filling.

Return pan to oven and bake on the top rack for 10 minutes or until the tips of the meringue are browned. Cool, then cut into 1 1/2-inch (4cm) squares.

Makes 25 squares.

Lemon Apricot Squares

Fruit is a vital part of many low-fat desserts. With its natural sweetness and healthful properties, it makes a nutritious diet not only easy, but tasty too.

1/4 cup (50ml)	soft butter
1 cup (250ml)	sugar
1/2 cup (125ml)	skim milk
1 tsp (5ml)	vanilla
1 1/4 cups (300ml)	all-purpose flour
1 1/2 tsp (7ml)	baking powder
1/4 tsp (1ml)	salt
1 tbsp (15ml)	lemon zest, finely grated
1 cup (250ml)	apricot preserves

Preheat oven to 350ºF (180ºC).

Cream together butter and sugar. Beat in milk and vanilla.

In a separate bowl, mix together flour, baking powder, and salt. Stir in lemon zest. Stir flour mixture into creamed mixture in thirds. Spread dough in a lightly-greased 8-inch (2L) square pan,

Bake on middle rack of the oven for 30 minutes or until a toothpick comes out clean. Let cool then spread with apricot preserves and cut into 1 1/2-inch (4cm) squares.

Makes 25 squares.

Cherry Bombs

Fresh cherries explode with sweet flavour in this delicious cookie.

1/2 cup (125ml)	soft butter
1/2 cup (125ml)	sugar
1 tbsp (15ml)	honey
1	egg
2 tsp vanilla	
1 1/2 cups (375ml)	all-purpose flour
1/3 cup (75ml)	cornstarch
1/4 tsp (1ml)	baking powder
1/4 tsp (1ml)	baking soda
1/4 tsp (1ml)	salt
1/4 cup (50ml)	cherry preserves
36	cherries, pitted

Preheat oven to 375°F (190°C).

Cream together butter and sugar until light and fluffy. Beat in honey, egg, and vanilla. In a separate bowl, mix flour with cornstarch, baking powder, baking soda, and salt. Stir flour mixture into creamed butter in thirds.

Roll dough into scant 1-inch (2.5cm) balls and place 2 inches (5cm) apart on a greased cookie sheet. Press your thumb into the centre of each ball to make a small indentation. Spoon 1/4 tsp (1ml) jam into each indentation and press a cherry on top.

Bake on the middle rack of the oven for 8 minutes or until edges are golden. Transfer to cooling rack.

Makes 3 dozen cookies.

Skinny Pumpkin Cookies

Have you ever seen a skinny pumpkin? These cookies replace high-fat ingredients with plenty of spices and natural pumpkin taste.

3/4 cup (175ml)	canned unsweetened pumpkin
3/4 cup (175ml)	brown sugar, packed
1/2 cup (125ml)	low-fat yogurt
1	egg, beaten
1 tsp (5ml)	vanilla
1 cup (250ml)	golden raisins
2 cups (500ml)	pastry flour
2 tsp (10ml)	cinnamon
1/2 tsp (2ml)	ground ginger
1/4 tsp (1ml)	freshly ground nutmeg
1/2 tsp (2ml)	baking soda
1/4 tsp (1ml)	salt

Preheat oven to 350ºF (180ºC).

In a large stainless steel or glass bowl, stir together pumpkin, sugar, yogurt, egg, vanilla, and raisins. In a separate bowl, combine flour, cinnamon, ginger, nutmeg, baking soda, and salt.

Stir flour mixture into pumpkin mixture in thirds. Drop half-tablespoons of dough 2 inches (5cm) apart on a parchment-lined cookie sheet.

Bake for 12 to 15 minutes or until set. Transfer to cooling racks.

Makes about 3 dozen cookies.

Banana Mango Cookies

Fresh and dried fruits are the order of the day for these tropical morsels.

1/2 cup (125ml)	packed brown sugar
1/2 cup (125ml)	liquid honey
2 cups (500ml)	mashed bananas
2 tbsp (25ml)	canola oil
1	egg
1 tbsp (15ml)	vanilla
3/4 cup (175ml)	chopped dried mango
2 1/2 cups (625ml)	quick-cooking oats
2 cups (500ml)	pastry flour
1 tsp (5ml)	baking powder
2 tsp (10ml)	cinnamon
1/4 tsp (1ml)	salt

Preheat oven to 350ºF (180ºC).

In a large bowl, beat together sugar, honey, bananas, oil, egg, and vanilla. Stir in mango and oats. In a separate bowl, mix together flour, baking powder, cinnamon, and salt.

Stir flour mixture into liquid ingredients. Drop heaping tablespoons of dough 2 inches (5cm) apart onto a parchment-lined cookie sheet.

Bake on the middle rack of the oven for 12 to 15 minutes or until golden. Transfer to cooling racks.

Makes about 2 dozen cookies.

Meringue Chocolate Chip Cookies

This recipe could have been included in the chapter on chocolate chip cookies, but the concept of a low-fat chocolate chip cookie is so delicious, I had to highlight it here.

2	egg whites
Pinch	cream of tartar
1/2 cup (125ml)	sugar
1 tsp (5ml)	vanilla
1/2 tsp (2ml)	cinnamon
1/2 cup (125ml)	pastry flour
1/2 cup (125ml)	chocolate chips
2 tsp (10ml)	grated lemon zest

Preheat oven to 250ºF (120ºC).

In a clean stainless steel, glass or copper-lined bowl, whip egg whites with a pinch of cream of tartar on low speed until they begin to hold their shape. Increase speed to medium and gradually whip in sugar until stiff peaks form. Whip in vanilla and cinnamon. Fold in flour, chocolate chips, and lemon zest.

Drop heaping teaspoons of dough 2 inches (5cm) apart on a cookie sheet lined with greased parchment.

Bake for 30 minutes. Turn off heat and leave cookies in the oven for 30 minutes to cool and set.

Makes about 2 dozen cookies.

Cinnamon Applesauce Cookies

Applesauce replaces half of the butter normally used in this type of recipe.
To lower fat still further, keep the yield and portions small.

3 tbsp (50ml)	butter
3 tbsp (50ml)	sugar
1	egg white
1 tsp (5ml)	vanilla
3 tbsp (50ml)	applesauce
2/3 cup (150ml)	all-purpose flour
1 tsp (5ml)	cinnamon
1/2 tsp (2ml)	baking powder
Pinch	salt

GARNISH

1 tsp (5ml)	sugar
1/2 tsp (2ml)	cinnamon
1	egg white, lightly beaten

Cream together butter and sugar. Beat in egg, vanilla, and applesauce.

In a separate bowl, mix together flour, cinnamon, baking powder, and salt. Stir flour mixture into applesauce mixture in thirds. Refrigerate for 1 hour.

Preheat oven to 375ºF (190ºC).

Between two sheets of plastic or parchment, roll out to 1/8-inch (3mm) thickness. Cut out shapes with 1-inch (2.5cm) cookie cutters and place on parchment-lined cookie sheet. Mix together sugar and cinnamon. Brush cookies with egg white and dust with sweet cinnamon.

Bake on the middle rack of the oven for 16 to 18 minutes.

Makes about 2 dozen cookies.

Ginger Morsels

These cookies are a little messy to make but
they can't be beaten for low-fat taste.

1/3 cup (75ml)	soft butter
1 cup (250ml)	packed brown sugar
1/4 cup (50ml)	buttermilk
2	egg whites
1 tsp (5ml)	vanilla
2 3/4 cups (675ml)	all-purpose flour
1 tsp (5ml)	cinnamon
1/2 tsp (2ml)	baking powder
1/4 tsp (1ml)	salt
1/4 tsp (1ml)	ground ginger
1 cup (250ml)	ginger marmalade

Preheat oven to 400ºF (200ºC).

Cream together butter and sugar until light and fluffy. Beat in buttermilk, egg whites, and vanilla.

In a separate bowl, combine flour, cinnamon, baking powder, salt, and ginger. Stir flour mixture into creamed mixture in thirds.

Drop teaspoons of dough 2 inches (5cm) apart on a parchment-lined cookie sheet. Top with 1/2 tsp (2ml) marmalade, then cover with 1/2 tsp (2ml) dough.

Bake on the middle rack of the oven for 10 minutes or until golden. Transfer to cooling racks.

Makes about 4 dozen cookies.

Banana Hazelnut Squares

Mashed bananas are a boon to the low-fat cook. They contribute flavour, moisture, and tenderness to baked goods without adding fat.

2 tbsp (25ml)	softened butter
2/3 cup (150ml)	sugar
1/2 cup (125ml)	low-fat sour cream
2	egg whites
2	medium bananas, mashed
1 tsp (5ml)	vanilla
1 cup (250ml)	all-purpose flour
1/2 tsp (2ml)	baking soda
1/4 tsp (1ml)	freshly ground nutmeg
1 cup (250ml)	low-fat spreadable cream cheese
2 tbsp (25ml)	ground hazelnuts

Preheat oven to 375ºF (190ºC).

Cream together butter and sugar until light and fluffy. Beat in sour cream, egg whites, bananas, and vanilla.

In a separate bowl, combine flour, baking soda, and nutmeg. Stir flour mixture into liquid ingredients until incorporated. Spread into greased 8-inch (2L) square baking pan.

Bake on the middle rack of the oven for 20 minutes or until golden.

Once cool, spread cream cheese over top, dust with hazelnuts, and cut into 1 1/2-inch squares.

Makes 25 squares.

Date Almond Bonbons

Dates bring more than their natural sweetness to this dessert;
they are also a source of iron and protein.

4 oz (100g)	semi-sweet chocolate
2 cups (500ml)	pitted dates
1/2 cup (125ml)	ground almonds
2 tbsp (25ml)	almond (or other nut) liqueur
2 tbsp (25ml)	honey
1/4 cup (50ml)	cocoa
36	small paper cups

Melt chocolate in a double boiler or stainless steel bowl over hot (not boiling) water. Finely chop dates and combine with almonds, liqueur, and honey. Stir in all but 1 tbsp (15ml) of melted chocolate.

Keeping your hands moist with cold water, roll date mixture into 3/4-inch (2cm) balls. Dredge each ball in cocoa and place in a small paper cup. Dip the end of a knife in the remaining melted chocolate and drizzle a fine line over bonbons to decorate. Store in refrigerator.

Makes about 3 dozen cookies.

Lower-Fat Fig Walnut Squares

This recipe cannot quite be classified as low-fat, but it is a more healthful option for such a delicious treat.

			FILLING	
			1 cup (250ml)	walnuts
1/2 cup (125ml)	all-purpose flour		2/3 cup (150ml)	packed brown sugar
3/4 tsp (4ml)	baking powder		2	eggs
1/4 tsp (1ml)	salt		2	egg whites
2 tbsp (25ml)	butter		1/4 cup (50ml)	golden syrup
1/2 cup (125ml)	oats		1 tbsp (15ml)	melted butter
3 tbsp (50ml)	milk		2 tsp (10ml)	vanilla
			1/3 cup (75ml)	chopped dried figs

Preheat oven to 375ºF (190ºC).

In a medium bowl, combine flour, baking powder, and salt. Rub in butter until incorporated. Grind oats in a food processor, then stir into flour mixture. Stir in milk, 1 tbsp (15ml) at a time, until dough just comes together. Press into a greased 8-inch (2L) square pan.

Toast walnuts on a baking sheet for 8 minutes. Set aside to cool.

Cream together brown sugar, eggs, and egg whites until mixture is light and creamy. Stir in syrup, butter, vanilla, figs, and half of the cooled walnuts. Pour filling into crust and top with remaining walnuts.

Bake for 25 minutes or until crust is golden and filling is set. Let cool, then cut into 1 1/2-inch (4cm) squares.

Makes 25 squares.

Cherry Delights

*Cherries have been the icing on the cake since their
first recorded appearance, around 300 BC.*

1/3 cup (75ml)	dried cherries
2 tbsp (25ml)	orange liqueur
1/4 cup (50ml)	soft butter
1/4 cup (50ml)	packed brown sugar
1	egg
1 tbsp (15ml)	honey
1 tsp (5ml)	vanilla
3/4 cup (175ml)	all-purpose flour
1 tsp (5ml)	baking powder
Pinch	salt
2/3 cup (150ml)	cornmeal

Preheat oven to 350ºF (180ºC).

In a small pan over low heat, warm the cherries in orange liqueur until all the liquid is absorbed. Set aside to cool.

Cream together butter and sugar until light and fluffy. Beat in egg, then honey and vanilla. In a separate bowl, combine flour, baking powder, and salt. Stir in cornmeal.

Add cooled cherries to the creamed mixture, then stir in flour mixture in thirds. Roll dough into 1-inch (2.5cm) balls, place on a parchment-lined cookie sheet, and flatten slightly

Bake on the middle rack of the oven for 12 minutes or until golden. Transfer to wire racks to cool.

Makes about 2 dozen cookies.

Everybody Loves a Square

Squares are a fantastic treat, both for the baker and for the lucky guest who is invited to taste them. I find squares are even easier to make than cookies, since there is no shaping involved. Usually the batter is poured into a baking dish, baked, cooled, and then cut into bite-sized pieces.

The brownie, like the chocolate chip cookie, has found a place in our hearts and you can never go wrong presenting a plate of these chocolatey squares, so I just don't think it's possible to have too many brownie recipes. Three types of brownies are featured in this chapter

This chapter also includes other old favourites along with some delicious ideas that may be new to you. Try the Sweet Polenta Squares or experiment with the taste of elderflowers. The recipes on the following pages will guide you, and the results are certain to please.

Brownies

This treat — named after Scottish household fairies —
will make a welcome reward after a hard day's work.

3 oz (75g)	semi-sweet chocolate
1/3 cup (75ml)	butter
1/2 cup (125ml)	all-purpose flour
1/2 tsp (2ml)	baking powder
2	eggs
1 cup (250ml)	sugar
1 cup (250ml)	chopped walnuts

Preheat oven to 325ºF (160ºC).

In a double boiler or stainless steel bowl over hot (not boiling) water, melt chocolate and butter. Cool slightly.

Sift together flour and baking powder. Whip eggs until frothy, then beat in sugar. Stir chocolate into eggs. Stir flour into chocolate mixture, then fold in walnuts. Spread batter evenly over a greased and floured 8-inch (2-L) square pan.

Bake on the middle rack of the oven for 20 to 25 minutes or until the edges pull away from the sides of the pan. Cut into 2-inch (5cm) squares while still hot.

Makes 16 squares.

White-Chocolate Macadamia Brownies

Because macadamia nuts have a high fat content, they will go rancid quickly.
Buy them in small amounts, store in the refrigerator, and use within a few days.
These brownies are also best eaten within a day or two of baking.

4 oz (125g)	semisweet chocolate
1/2 cup (125ml)	butter
1 1/4 cups (300ml)	sugar
1 tsp (5ml)	vanilla
1/4 tsp (1ml)	salt
2	eggs
3/4 cup (175ml)	all-purpose flour
1/2 tsp (2ml)	baking powder
2/3 cup (150ml)	chopped macadamia nuts
1 cup (250ml)	white chocolate chips

Preheat oven to 325ºF (160ºC).

In a double boiler or stainless steel bowl over hot (not boiling) water, melt the semisweet chocolate with the butter. Remove from heat. Stir sugar, vanilla, and salt into chocolate. Beat in eggs, one at a time, and mix on low speed until the chocolate mixture is light and creamy.

In a separate bowl, combine flour and baking powder. Stir into chocolate mixture in thirds. Fold in nuts and white chocolate chips. Pour batter into a foil-lined 8-inch (2L) square baking pan.

Bake for 40 to 45 minutes or until the top springs back to the touch. Cool, then cut into 2-inch (5cm) squares.

Makes 16 squares.

Moccachino Brownies

Chocolate and espresso wins hands down as my favourite flavour combination. These days it's easy enough to pop down to a specialty coffee shop for a shot of espresso, but if need be, regular java can be substituted.

8 oz (250g)	semisweet chocolate		
3/4 cup (175ml)	butter		
3	eggs		
1 1/4 cups (300ml)	sugar	**FROSTING**	
2 tbsp (25ml)	strong, brewed, espresso coffee	6 oz (170g)	semi sweet chocolate
		2 tbsp (25ml)	butter
1 tbsp (15ml)	vanilla	2 tbsp (25ml)	strong, brewed espresso coffee
1 cup (250ml)	almonds, chopped		
1 cup (250ml)	all-purpose flour	1/2 cup (125ml)	whipping cream
1 tsp (5ml)	cinnamon		
1/4 tsp (1ml)	salt		

Preheat oven to 350ºF (180ºC).

In a double boiler or stainless steel bowl over hot (not boiling) water, melt chocolate and butter. In a separate bowl, beat eggs and sugar together until mixture is light and ribbons form. Stir in chocolate mixture, then coffee, vanilla, and almonds.

Combine flour, cinnamon and salt. Stir flour mixture into chocolate mixture in thirds. Pour into a greased and floured 9x13-inch (3.5L) baking dish.

Bake on the middle rack of the oven for 35 minutes or until the top springs back to the touch. Place pan on cooling rack.

To make the frosting, melt chocolate and butter in a double boiler or stainless steel bowl over hot (not boiling) water. Whisk in coffee and cream until smooth. Spread over cooled brownies. Let frosting set, then cut into 2-inch (5cm) squares.

Makes 2 dozen squares.

Honey-Roasted Cashew Squares

Granola comes in many varieties, but any type will work for this recipe.

3/4 cup (175ml)	cold butter
1 1/2 cups (375ml)	all-purpose flour
1/4 cup (50ml)	packed brown sugar

TOPPING

1 cup (250ml)	liquid honey
2/3 cup (150ml)	packed brown sugar
2	eggs
1 cup (250ml)	granola
1/2 cup (125ml)	honey-roasted cashews, ground
1/4 cup (50ml)	flour

Preheat oven to 350ºF (180ºC).

Rub butter into flour until the texture resembles coarse meal. Stir in sugar. Press into an ungreased 8-inch (2L) baking pan.

Bake on the middle rack of the oven for 15 minutes or until partially baked.

In a small pan over medium heat, stir together honey and sugar for 5 minutes. Beat eggs in a medium stainless steel or glass bowl. Slowly whisk in hot sugar mixture. In a separate bowl, combine granola, cashews, and flour, then stir into the liquid ingredients. Pour topping over partially-baked pastry

Bake for 20 minutes or until set. Cool, then cut into 2-inch (5cm) squares.

Makes 16 squares.

Cheesecake Squares

Cheesecake cracks if it is overbaked or if it is moved too quickly from a hot oven to room temperature. Check your squares after the first 20 minutes. If they are set around the edges and just a little loose in the centre, it's time to turn off the oven.

2/3 cup (150ml)	butter
1 1/2 cups (375ml)	graham cracker crumbs
1 1/2 oz (40g)	semisweet chocolate
8 oz (250g)	soft cream cheese
1/4 cup (50ml)	sugar
1	egg
2 tbsp (25ml)	sour cream
1 tbsp (15ml)	lemon juice
1 tsp (5ml)	vanilla

Preheat oven to 350ºF (180ºC).

Rub butter into graham crackers until fully incorporated. Press into a greased 8-inch (2L) square pan.

In a double boiler or stainless steel bowl over hot (not boiling) water, melt chocolate.

Beat the cream cheese and sugar together until the mixture is light and ribbons form. Beat in egg, then sour cream, lemon juice, and vanilla.

Spread the cheese mixture over the graham cracker layer. Drizzle melted chocolate from a spoon over the cheese layer and swirl the chocolate.

Bake on the middle rack of the oven for 20 to 25 minutes or until edges are golden.

Turn off heat, prop the oven door open, and leave cake to cool for 15 minutes. Remove from oven and finish cooling on a rack. Cut cooled cheesecake into 2-inch (5cm) squares.

Makes 16 squares.

Polenta Squares

*Polenta plays a central role in northern Italian cuisine. It can be
made into desserts such as these squares, but it is often served as a savoury dish.
Polenta can be cooked with parmesan or gorgonzola cheese, and either served
hot and creamy or left to cool, cut into shapes, and sautéed.
Whole books have been written on how to cook this versatile food.*

3 cups (750ml)	milk
1/2 cup (125ml)	sugar
1 cup (250ml)	cornmeal
1	egg, beaten
4	egg yolks, beaten
1/4 cup (50ml)	soft butter
1/4 cup (50ml)	hazelnuts, ground
1/4 cup (50ml)	finely grated lemon zest
2 tbsp (25ml)	graham cracker crumbs
2 tbsp (25ml)	powdered sugar
1 tbsp (15ml)	cocoa
1 tsp (5ml)	cinnamon

Preheat oven to 350ºF (180ºC).

In a medium saucepan over medium heat, combine milk and sugar and bring to a simmer. Whisk in eggs. Add cornmeal in a thin stream, whisking constantly. Reduce heat to low and cook, stirring constantly, for 5 minutes or until thick and creamy. Stir in butter, hazelnuts, and lemon zest.

Dust a greased 8-inch (2L) square pan with graham cracker crumbs and pour in polenta.

Bake for 20 minutes on the middle rack of the oven.

Combine powdered sugar, cocoa and cinnamon, and dust over the top of the baked polenta. Cut into 1 1/2-inch (4cm) squares. Serve warm or cold.

Makes 25 squares.

Elderflower Squares

*Elderflowers can be difficult to obtain, but if you have a source,
try these delicious squares. If you cannot find fresh elderflowers,
look for the dried variety in health-food or specialty stores.*

2	egg yolks
1/2 cup (125ml)	sugar
1/2 cup (125ml)	soft butter
1 cup (250ml)	all-purpose flour
1 1/2 cups (375ml)	cornmeal
2 tsp (10ml)	baking powder
1 tbsp (15ml)	lemon zest, minced
1 tsp (5ml)	elderflowers, minced
1/4 tsp	salt
1/2 cup (125ml)	elderflower beverage or milk
1/4 cup (50ml)	ground almonds
1/4 cup (50ml)	powdered sugar

Preheat oven to 350°F (180°C).

Beat together egg yolks and sugar until light and creamy. Beat in butter. In a separate bowl, combine flour, cornmeal, baking powder, lemon zest, elderflowers, and salt.

Stir flour mixture into butter mixture in thirds, alternating with elderflower beverage. Pour batter into a greased and floured 8-inch (2L) square pan.

Bake on the middle rack of the oven for 35 minutes or until golden.

Let cool, then dust with ground almonds and powdered sugar. Cut into 1 1/2-inch (4cm) squares.

Makes 25 squares.

Date and Chestnut Cake

*Look for chestnut flour in Italian markets. Its unique, delicate flavour
can be used to enhance the character of many baked goods.*

1 1/2 cups (375ml)	pastry flour
1 1/2 cups (375ml)	chestnut flour
1/2 cup (125ml)	sugar
1 tsp (5ml)	baking powder
1/4 tsp (1ml)	salt
1/4 cup (50ml)	chopped dates
1/4 cup (50ml)	hazelnuts, chopped
2 1/2 cups (625ml)	milk
2 tbsp (25ml)	butter, melted
1	egg

Preheat oven to 350º (180ºC).

Combine pastry flour, chestnut flour, sugar, baking powder, and salt. Stir in dates and hazelnuts.

In a separate bowl, beat together milk, melted butter, and egg. Make a well in the flour mixture
and pour in the liquid ingredients. Stir until the dough just comes together. Pour into a greased
9x13-inch (3.5L) baking dish.

Bake on the middle rack of the oven for 30 to 35 minutes or until the top springs back to the
touch. Let cool, then cut into 1 1/2-inch (4cm) squares.

Makes 25 squares.

Maple-Pecan Squares

Serve these squares with maple-pecan ice cream on the side.

2/3 cup (150ml)	soft butter
1/2 cup (125ml)	sugar
1 1/2 cups (375ml)	all-purpose flour

FILLING

3	eggs
1/3 cup (75ml)	packed brown sugar
1 cup (250ml)	maple syrup
1 tsp (5ml)	vinegar
1 tsp (5ml)	vanilla
3 tbsp (50ml)	butter, melted
1 cup (250ml)	pecans

Preheat oven to 350°F (180°C).

Cream together butter and sugar until light and fluffy. Stir in flour in thirds.

Press into an ungreased 9-inch (2.5L) baking pan.

Bake on the middle rack of the oven for 13 to 15 minutes or until golden. Remove pan from oven and increase heat to 375°F (190°C).

Prepare the filling. Beat eggs until foamy, then beat in sugar until creamy. Beat in syrup, vinegar, and vanilla until smooth, then mix in melted butter. Spread pecans evenly over bottom of baked base, then cover with filling.

Bake on the lower rack of the oven for 25 minutes or until edges are set. Let cool and cut into 1 1/2-inch (4cm) squares.

Makes 36 squares.

Linzer Squares

*Linzertorte is an Austrian dessert that has become a Canadian classic.
I enjoy it most when it is made with homemade raspberry preserves.*

1 cup (250ml)	soft butter
1 cup (250ml)	sugar
1	large egg
1 tsp (5ml)	vanilla
1 1/2 cups (375ml)	ground hazelnuts
2 cups (500ml)	all-purpose flour
1 tsp (5ml)	baking soda
1 cup (250ml)	raspberry jam

Preheat oven to 350°F (180°C).

Cream together butter and sugar until light and fluffy. Beat in egg, then vanilla. Stir in hazelnuts.

In a separate bowl, combine flour and baking soda. Stir flour mixture into creamed mixture in thirds. Press two-thirds of the dough into a greased and floured 13x9-inch (3.5L) baking pan.

Bake on the middle rack of the oven for 20 minutes or until golden.

Remove pan from oven, spread jam over the crust, and crumble remaining dough on top. Return pan to the oven and bake for 20 minutes or until golden. Cool completely before cutting into 2-inch (5cm) squares.

Makes 2 dozen squares.

Date Walnut Squares

Buy chopped dates to save the extra job of cutting them up —
it's usually a sticky mess.

FILLING

2 cups (500ml)	chopped dates
1/2 cup (125ml)	water
1 tbsp (15ml)	lemon juice
1/4 cup (50ml)	chopped walnuts

BASE

1 1/2 cups (375ml)	all-purpose flour
1/2 tsp (2ml)	baking soda
1/2 tsp (2ml)	baking powder
1/4 tsp (1ml)	salt
1 cup (250ml)	cold butter, cubed
1 cup (250ml)	quick-cooking oats
1 cup (250ml)	packed brown sugar

Preheat oven to 325°F (160°C).

In a medium, nonreactive pan over medium heat, combine dates, water, and lemon juice and cook until thick, about 3 to 5 minutes. Stir in walnuts and set aside to cool.

In a large bowl, combine flour, baking soda, baking powder, and salt. Rub in butter until the texture resembles coarse meal. Stir in oats and brown sugar.

Press three-quarters of the dough into a greased 9-inch (2.5L) square pan. Spread cooled date mixture over dough, and crumble remaining dough over top.

Bake on the middle rack of the oven for 30 minutes. Increase temperature to 350°F (180°C) and bake for an additional 15 minutes or until golden. Cut into 1 1/2-inch (4cm) squares and let cool.

Makes 3 dozen squares.

Date Fingers

*Squares, like cookies, should be cooled on a rack so
that the heat can dissipate quickly and evenly. As long as
the squares are hot, they continue to cook.*

2	eggs, separated
Pinch	cream of tartar
1 cup (250ml)	confectioners' sugar
1 tsp (5ml)	vanilla
2/3 cup (150ml)	flour
1 tsp (5ml)	baking powder
1 cup (250ml)	pitted dates, chopped
1/2 cup (125ml)	pistachios, chopped

Preheat oven to 325°F (160°C).

Beat egg whites with cream of tartar until firm. Beat egg yolks with sugar and vanilla until light and fluffy. Fold whites into yolks.

In a separate bowl, sift together flour and baking powder, then fold into the egg mixture. Fold in dates and pistachios. Spread into a greased 9-inch (2.5L) baking pan.

Bake on the middle rack of the oven for 25 minutes or until set and golden. Let cool, then cut into 1 1/2x2-inch (4x5cm) fingers.

Makes about 3 dozen fingers.

Sunflower Bars

If you cannot find honey-roasted sunflower seeds,
use the plain-roasted variety and dust with powdered sugar
after you sprinkle them on the squares.

1/4 cup (50ml)	soft butter
3/4 cup (175ml)	sugar
1	egg
1 tbsp (15ml)	milk
1 tsp (5ml)	vanilla
1 tsp (5ml)	lemon extract
2 cups (500ml)	all-purpose flour
1 tsp (5ml)	baking powder
1/4 tsp (1ml)	salt
1/2 cup (125ml)	honey-roasted sunflower seeds
1	egg white, beaten

Preheat oven to 375ºF (190ºC).

Cream together butter and sugar until light and fluffy. Beat in egg, milk, vanilla, and lemon extract.

In a separate bowl, combine flour, baking powder, salt and 1/4 cup (50ml) of the sunflower seeds. Stir flour mixture into creamed mixture in thirds.

Between two sheets of waxed paper, roll out dough to 1/4-inch (5mm) thickness. Cut into 2 1/2x1-inch (8x2.5cm) bars, and place on a parchment-lined cookie sheet. Brush bars with egg white and dust with sunflower seeds.

Bake on the middle rack of the oven for 12 to 15 minutes or until golden. Transfer to cooling racks.

Makes about 3 dozen bars.

Chocolate Walnut Bars

Melt the chocolate gently over hot water. If the water is boiling, the chocolate will become dull and grainy.

2	eggs
1 cup (250ml)	sugar
1/2 cup (125ml)	butter, melted
1 tsp (5ml)	vanilla
3/4 cup (175ml)	flour
2 tbsp (25ml)	cocoa
1/2 tsp (2ml)	baking powder
1 cup (250ml)	walnuts, chopped
3 oz (75g)	semi-sweet chocolate
2 tbsp (25ml)	whipping cream

Preheat oven to 350ºF (180ºC).

In a large bowl, whip eggs until light. Beat in sugar, butter, and vanilla.

In a separate bowl, combine flour, cocoa, and baking powder. Stir into liquid ingredients in thirds. Fold in walnuts. Pour batter into a greased 8-inch (2L) pan.

Bake on the middle rack of the oven for 10 to 15 minutes or until the edges pull away from the sides of the pan. Set aside to cool.

Melt chocolate in a double boiler or stainless steel bowl over hot (not boiling) water. Stir in cream and pour over cooled squares. Cut into 1 1/2-inch (4cm) squares.

Makes 25 squares.

Anise Bars

*If you cannot find anise oil, substitute peppermint.
To intensify the anise flavour, dust 1 tsp (5ml) of anise
seeds over the top with the poppy seeds.*

1/4 cup (50ml)	soft butter
3/4 cup (175ml)	sugar
2	eggs
2 drops	anise oil
2 cups (500ml)	all-purpose flour
1 tsp (5ml)	baking powder
1/4 tsp (1ml)	salt
1	egg white, slightly beaten
3 tbsp (50ml)	poppy seeds

Preheat oven to 325ºF (160ºC).

Cream together butter and sugar. Beat in eggs, one at a time, then anise oil.

In a separate bowl, combine flour, baking powder, and salt. Stir flour mixture into creamed mixture in thirds. Press into a greased 8-inch (2L) square pan. Brush top with egg white and dust with poppy seeds.

Bake on the middle rack of the oven for 12 to 15 minutes or until firm. Let cool, then cut into 1x1 1/2-inch (4x5cm) bars.

Makes 35 bars.

Buttered-Almond Fudge Bars

*When melting chocolate, the water in the double boiler or under
the stainless steel bowl should be just hot enough to melt the chocolate slowly,
but not hot enough to simmer. If the water under the melting chocolate
is too hot, the chocolate will become grainy and dull.*

1/2 cup (125ml)	soft butter
1 cup (250ml)	sugar
1	egg
1 tsp (5ml)	vanilla
6 oz (170ml)	semi-sweet chocolate
1 1/2 cups (375ml)	pastry flour
1 tsp (5ml)	baking powder
1/4 tsp (1ml)	salt
2 tbsp (25ml)	whipping cream
1/3 cup (75ml)	buttered almonds

Preheat oven to 400ºF (200ºC).

Cream together butter and sugar until light and fluffy. Beat in egg and vanilla.

Melt chocolate in a double boiler or a stainless steel bowl over hot (not boiling) water. Beat one third of the chocolate into the creamed mixture. Set remaining chocolate aside.

In a separate bowl, combine flour, baking powder, and salt. Stir flour mixture into chocolate mixture in thirds. Press dough into a greased 8-inch (2L) square pan.

Bake on the middle rack of the oven for 20 minutes or until set. Leave to cool.

Warm reserved chocolate over hot water until soft, and stir in whipping cream. Pour over squares and sprinkle top with buttered almonds. When chocolate topping is set, cut into 2-inch (5cm) squares.

Makes 16 squares.

Pine-Nut and Currant Squares

We usually associate pine nuts with pesto and savory dishes, but this flavourful nut is also wonderful in baked goods. Pine nuts are expensive because they are difficult to extract from pine cones. They are also high in fat and will become rancid quickly, so buy them small quantities and store them in the refrigerator.

1/2 cup (125ml)	cold butter, cubed
1 cup (250ml)	flour
2 tbsp (25ml)	sugar
Pinch	salt

FILLING

1 1/2 cups (375ml)	brown sugar
3 tbsp (50ml)	flour
1/4 tsp (1ml)	salt
3	eggs, beaten
1 tsp (5ml)	vanilla
1/2 cup (125ml)	currants
1 cup (250ml)	pine nuts

Preheat oven to 350°F (180°C).

Rub butter into flour until the texture resembles coarse meal. Stir in sugar and salt. Press into a 8-inch (2L) square pan .

Bake for 15 minutes or until firm.

Meanwhile, make the filling. Stir together brown sugar, flour, and salt. Add pine nuts and currants. Stir in eggs and vanilla. Spread filling evenly over cooked base.

Return pan to oven and bake for 20 to 25 minutes or until browned and set, but still loose in the centre. Let cool then cut into 16 squares.

Makes 16 squares.

Bibliography

Armstrong, Julian. *A Taste of Quebec*. Toronto: Macmillan of Canada, 1990.

Baird, Elizabeth. *Classic Canadian Cooking: Menus for the Seasons*. Toronto: James Lorimer,1974.

A Blue Flame Kitchen™ Holiday Collection: 75th Anniversary Commemorative Edition (Edmonton: ATCO Gas, 1998)

Davidson, Alan. *The Oxford Companion to Food*. Oxford: Oxford University Press, 1999.

Herbst, Sharon Tyler. *The New Food Lover's Companion*. Second edition. Hauppauge, New York: Barron's Educational Series, 1995.

Labensky, Sarah R., et al. *On Cooking: A Textbook of Culinary Fundamentals*. Canadian edition. Scarborough, Ontario: Prentice Hall, 1999.

McGee, Harold. *On Food and Cooking: The Science and Lore of the Kitchen*. New York: Scribner, 1984; New York: Collier, 1988.

Mongrain-Dontigny, Micheline. *Traditional Quebec Cooking: A Treasure of Heirloom Recipes*. La Tuque, Québec: Les éditions La bonne recette, 1995.

Montagné, Prosper. *Larousse Gastronomique: The New American Edition of the World's Greatest Culinary Encyclopedia*. Edited by Jenifer Harvey Long. New York: Crown, 1988.

Murray, Rose. *Rose Murray's Comfortable Kitchen Cookbook*. Toronto: McGraw-Hill Ryerson, 1991.

Sonnenfeld, Albert. *Food: A Culinary History from Antiquity to the present*. Under the direction of Jean-Louis Flandrin and Massimo Montanari. English edition. New York: Columbia University Press, 1999.

Index